ERRATA

The publisher and author would like to apologize for the errors that appear in the following pages. None of these are their fault, and the printer gets off clean as well. The guilty will be found and punished in later editions.

Page 31: The 2000 Year Old Man routine was dead on arrival, but unfortunately not discovered until almost one millennium later.

Page 33: Last paragraph, third line, should read: "Is it closer to Portland, or by bus?"

Page 64: Replace "Luciano Pavarotti" with "Andrea Bocelli."

Page 67: In the revised *To Kill a Mockingbird*, steel shot replaces lead in the older shotgun shells. For a rough equivalent, go one size larger steel shot.

Page 78: Under fishy literary politics, it's "Salman," not "Salmon" Rushdie.

Page 87: If an angel touches you there, notify the authorities.

Page 89: Replace "sweet butter" with "any familiar brand of margarine or suet."

Page 91: Gentle Ben is not even remotely related to Big Ben.

Page 103: To cook a feral cat, bake at 250 degrees for 4 hours, not 4 degrees for 250 hours.

Page 105: Most of the charges were later dropped. This was thought to be an egregious error.

Page 111: The hair dryer should be set on low.

Page 145: The total amount of rice-based beer that any amphibian can drink and still drive in a one-hour period is two (2) ounces, not cases.

Page 164: Will the last one turning the page please turn off the lights?

Page 201: The heading should read, "Pet Genitals That Look Like Their Owners."

WILDLIFE

OF THE

NEW MILLENNIUM

A Field Guide

Buck Peterson

Illustrations by J. Angus "Sourdough" McLean

Longstreet Press
Marietta, Georgia

Published by LONGSTREET PRESS, INC., A subsidiary of Cox Newspapers, A subsidiary of Cox Enterprises, Inc. 2140 Newmarket Parkway, Suite 122, Marietta, Georgia 30067, www.lspress.com

Printed in the USA
First printing, 1999
Library of Congress Catalog Card Number: 99-61763
ISBN: 1-56352-546-1

Set in 10/12 Diddywahdiddy

Cover artwork © 1999 by J. Angus "Sourdough" McLean
Illustrations by J. Angus "Sourdough" McLean

For Nicole

Contents

We can never have enough nature.
—Henry David Thoreau,
Walden "Spring"

Bet me!
—Animal Control Officer,
Walden Pond View Estates

INTRODUCTION

ARMED WITH traditional guidebooks, more and more city folks are taking to the field as wildlife watchers for their first personal encounters with animals in a natural setting. With the dramatic growth and sprawl of urban populations into what was once wild lands, explorers need not go far afield for a zoo-like experience; their crabgrassed and rusted Weber-filled backyards are crawling with wild former occupants.

Traditional guidebooks do not prepare the well-appointed trekker for the behavioral changes and evolved characteristics of the residents of the scraped landscape. The charismatic megafauna now sighted on sweatshirts, bedding, and at species fundraisers are trying to adjust to our hyperactive multiple use of the outdoors and many, for good reason, are crossing the lines of acceptable behavior. These are their individual stories.

GENERAL
WILDLIFE
INFORMATION

OUR WILDLIFE

In the United States, a person is added every fourteen seconds, to the pop tune of over two million per year. Combined with legal and illegal immigration our population could swell from 265 million in 1997 to 400 million by 2050. We'll need over a million acres each year to accommodate these new citizens and by 2050, an area larger than the size of Louisiana will be needed to shelter, feed, and provide some kind of recreation for these pilgrims. The problem with all this is we don't have another Louisiana and if we did, we would see entirely too much of Emeril Lagasse and listen to way too much Beausoleil. By the end of the twenty-first century, the U.S. is expected to contain 500 million people; plan on a new Café Du Monde serving fresh beignets and chicory coffee sitting at the headwaters of the Mighty Mississippi as well.

The fastest growth is expected in the south and the west. Florida and Texas lead the south and California heads the western expansion. As the big states swell, adjoining states like Nevada, Colorado, and Georgia adjust accordingly and cities like Denver will do their best to cultivate big city-style graft to win an Olympics bid.

Left alone, this population growth wouldn't be such a concern because America's First Stewards of the Land would just build taller buildings. But as more and more Americans yearn to leave the city to get some elbow room, the first thing animals learn is that humans have very sharp elbows. The suburbs now contain 75 percent more families than the cities, and the population growth and sprawl on both sides of the suburbs translates into major animal habitat encroachment. Good citizens everywhere try to do the right thing by wearing gray wolf and Keiko sweatshirts, making little "wild-scapes" in small backyards, and buying bird feeders. Yet they still end up with animals who have NO MANNERS.

The urban sprawlers don't understand nature. The whitetail deer population was the first to risk domestication, just for the taste of farm-fresh sweet corn on the way to your rose bushes. From five hundred thousand deer at the turn of the century, there are now an estimated 20 million whitetails who prefer the relative safety of the new neighborhoods. Left alone, by the end of the twenty-first century the urban deer population will equal the number of people who, over the years, cried when Bambi lost his mom. By the end of the century, these deer will have eaten all the shrubs, small trees, decorative plants, and wood siding under ten feet in suburbia (not to speak of any vine-covered bridges on the way in).

If shortages of whitetail deer appear, the mountain lion population will adjust and follow an aging human population into the southwest. By 2050, over 18 million Americans will be over eighty-five and living in weakened states somewhere in the southwest or Florida. Once the Florida panther acquires a taste for this sun-dried meat, the cat's population will once again thrive.

WILD ANIMALS

The definition of what is a wild animal cannot be left to the behaviorists. You'll know one when you see one. There won't be any whites in their eyes, more like blood red with a crazed, agitated focus. When they blink, beat feet. Skedaddle. Hit the road. Scoot. Put the pedal to the metal. Look for the Louisville Slugger, Joe DiMaggio model.

There are several broad definitions of wild animals that will be useful for wildlife watching in the new millennium.

Original Native Animals

The animals that pre-date the arrival of the other first Native Americans are found only in picture books or fossil beds, or in southern Montana looking for the Ted Turner Bison Early Retirement Center.

Park Animals

Park animals are not wild, they are tame and confused, and you should listen to what they say about you after the guards go home. Park animals accept your food handouts, making them dependent on your visits, which disrupts their social life and concentrates their activities and population so you can run them over with your sport utility vehicle on the way back from the soccer match.

Endangered and Threatened Wild Animals

A threatened species is one likely to become endangered, and an endangered species is one in danger of becoming extinct in a large part or all of its former range. The federal government provides certain protections for each and a complete list is available from the World Wildlife Fund. A branch of the U.S. Internal Revenue Service provides tax benefits for those who set up private "Save Me" foundations for the most photogenic animals. The most endangered mammal is the one who understands the politics behind the detailed requirements of the Endangered Species Act and doesn't stretch the language for personal agendas.

Reintroduced Wild Animals

Gray wolves from Canada have been relocated in Yellowstone and there is a matching effort to reintroduce the Mexican gray wolf into New Mexico. The latter isn't doing as well as the former because there aren't alpha sheep in the former. Others wishing to recreate a historical wildlife model have or are reintroducing red wolves in North Carolina, and the lynx to New York's Adirondacks and Colorado's San Juan Mountains. There will be very few animals left in Canada unless the U.S. federal and state fish and wildlife services stop taking advantage of currency differences. The Canadian dollar is driving wildlife managers loony. Canadian wolves prefer the private U.S. veterinary system, especially the superior acute critical care for gunshot wounds.

The only successful reintroduction of an insect is the Volkswagen Beetle. It's hoped that Ford won't reopen their dusty aerie, home of the Falcon and the clipped-wing Thunderbird. Swimmers and town officials off Martha's Vineyard are hoping Disabled Friends of the Great White Shark won't reintroduce the predators blown up while making the early *Jaws* movies.

Invigorated Wild Animals

Some animals like fire ants prefer a disrupted landscape; others like whitetail deer prefer the "green belts" or strip habitat that a developer touts as a lifestyle amenity. The bald eagle, peregrine falcon, and the American alligator preferred being listed as endangered and

threatened. The Canada goose is now considered a nuisance in so many areas that the birds are being forcefully relocated to less populated areas. As anyone who has interacted with Canadian geese will understand, this assignment is best left to the most junior wildlife biologists.

Federal and state protection creates an environment (not habitat) that many animals find conducive to family life. Whitetail deer are so strong and healthy in their new suburban habitat that they have at least two, sometimes three, fawns in the spring. The wild horses of the Assateague Island National Seashore are horsing around so much that managers are trying immuno-contraception from the business end of a dart gun. If that doesn't work, a local priest will do a horse blanket conversion into the church known for its highly successful birth control positions. The best place to find an invigorated insect is in a New York City restaurant. Try the dumplings.

Wild Animals Yet To Be Discovered

It's unlikely there are wild animals yet to be discovered in the United States. The most recent mammal species to be uncovered is the Vietnamese barking deer, in which only the Smith Brothers have shown any commercial interest.

WHERE THEY LIVE

Animal Theme Parks, "Countries" and "Worlds"

Fenced tracts of land have become a popular way to see animals "interacting" according to script. Unlike zoos, animal parks rarely isolate the species and display a commercial version of biodiversity in larger habitats. They don't, however, dedicate the large acreage a mountain lion prefers, and the big cat stalking your hand hanging out the car window wants you to know that.

National Forests

The almost 200 million acres of forest under federal multiple-use management has historically tilted toward logging and spotted owl emergency care. In the last decade of the twentieth century, timbering has dropped substantially and the forest service now expects a billion recreational visits by the end of the first decade of the twenty-first century. Wildlife watching in national forests is for the hikers, as these animals aren't conditioned like national park animals to warily approach road traffic, especially any traffic that looks remotely like a logging truck.

National Parks

In the first decade of the twentieth century, there were only eleven national parks and the highest annual visitor count was 200,000. Now there are over 350 national park and recreation sites and 275 million visits were made in 1998,

the majority substantially below the lowest speed limits. If a bison is sighted, recreational vehicles travel at slightly above stall speed. If a bald eagle is sighted, the road ahead looks like an interstate pile-up.

Nature Centers/Wildlife Sanctuary

Often set up under the guise of a refuge for injured or orphaned animals, nature centers are where you'll find female mountain lions called Helen, bears named Rose and Ted, and humpback whales named Splash and Salt. The owners have an attractive lifestyle buoyed by the good nature of vacationers and subsidized by the lower taxes for nonprofit corporations. Centers and sanctuaries typically have more acreage dedicated to gift shops than to species habitat, but then again, "wild" animals from the lower orders are mixed with barnyard animals. Where they belong.

Wildlife Refuge

The national refuge system contains more than 550 units of 92 million acres stuffed full of wild animals. State and local refuges multiply these numbers substantially. Refuges are quite different than wildlife preserves. Pop a couple of caps in the air and you'll quickly know if you're in the latter—the local game warden will read you your rights for all your wrongs. If you accidentally harvest a wild animal during your experiment, you'll be placed in a wildlife preserve downtown.

Zoos

Originally the province of the rich, the best zoos are marketed as the equivalent of the Ark—preserving, studying, and breeding endangered species. The Ark didn't display any species, but Noah also didn't have to contend with society memberships and gate receipts. There was that minor drinking problem, though. Animals in small, fragmented habitats are not wild. They aren't tame, either. They're just zoo animals with zoo behavior, standing around. As the wildly painted bird in *Creature Comforts* (1990) notes, "animals don't have to do anything" in the zoo, seconded by the lion's complaints: "We don't like potatoes. We like fresh meat."

Mobile zoos offer animals opportunities to stretch their legs in The Greatest Show on Earth, yet for much less than the cost of bleacher seats, you can see many of the animals on the side of a box of animal crackers. The candy-coated crackers are best of all, but sugar gives animals worms so don't feed them to wild animals. Zoo animals, okay.

INTERACTION WITH WILDLIFE IN THE NEW MILLENNIUM

Extreme Sports

One of the fastest-growing paddle sports, sea kayaking intrudes on seals, sea otters, and orca and gray whales. Conflict with the sea otters can yield an unexpected bonus—burped fresh abalone. Conflict with the larger mammals and those who want to harpoon them is unwise. Whitewater kayaking is little threat to wildlife as no animal, except perhaps a young harlequin duck, is that crazy.

Mountain biking conflicts with trail-using mammals are mild skirmishes compared to the protracted wars between hikers, ATVers, and the back-country and dude ranch horse crowd.

Snowboarding rarely interferes with hibernat-ing animals. Mountain climbers rarely bother bighorn sheep, for the sim-ple reason that IMAX camera dollies do not fit on the ledges these high-country citizens travel.

The most modern and extreme interference with animals is orga-nized tramping through a specific species habitat, or eco-touring. While most of this rummaging about occurs overseas by those who wish to sit in trees and scratch mountain gorillas, or see for them-selves whether penguin evening wear is made by Armani, stateside tour operators offer individual sport packages modeled on the research techniques of wildlife biologists. One pilot program revolves around

9

mature anadromous fish, salmon that move from saltwater to fresh water to reproduce. Total immersion into such a cold-water species habitat affords the participants an important lesson in biodiversity. This technique of total immersion works well for Baptists, too, especially immersions lasting at least three minutes. Praise the Lord!

Non-Extreme Sports

The number-one human inactivity is golf, and the manicured lawns and ponds are magnets for herbivores and their predators. Golf course design creates an "edge" environment many animals have come to identify as safe, and golf course operations limit interruptions to animals feeding in the twilight hours. During the day, animals that can distinguish colors are at a loss for words when they see the golfer garb of the day. The horror, the sartorial horror.

Other popular human activities such as birding and hiking into the back country are not intrusive unless humans are inappropriate in some way. Sailing rarely puts marine animals at risk, and it takes a fully loaded sightseeing boat with two large inboard engines to move a humpback whale sideways.

Camping is an activity the whole wild kingdom can enjoy. A family fishing camp involves the lower orders (such as worms, insects, and leeches) and the higher orders (such as bears, mountain lions, and really big bears) with an appetite for picnic foods. Family vacations are held in all animal habitats—woodlands and grasslands, deserts and wetlands, streams, lakes, and ocean shores—and each is stuffed full of animals you don't know much about that are waiting for you to make just one mistake.

In the urban sprawl, the athletic can encounter all three types of animals—domesticated, feral, and wild—on morning and evening runs. If wild animal sounds coming from the shrubbery sound like a chuckle, they probably are. Less athletic city dwellers can expect significant vehicle-animal interaction to and from the workplace, health club, mall, and the "other woman." At work or play, the responsible citizen of the new millennium must recognize the inherent conflicts in the increasing numbers of interactions with the wild animals of the new realm.

CONFLICTS WITH WILDLIFE

General Areas of Conflict

Perceived versus real conflict with animals is a function of a particular animal's "carrying capacity." The cultural carrying capacity of an animal is the number the citizenry can tolerate. One deer eating Twinkies from your child's hand may be cute, but a herd of them stripping your rose bushes is not.

The biological or ecological carrying capacity is the number of animals an area can support in terms of food, shelter, and other resources, or how many Canada geese can one eighteen-hole golf course support.

Human carrying capacity is the number of people at home, play, or on vacation that the land can support. Add the notion of sustainable development that meets present needs without affecting ability of future generations to meet their needs, explosive population growth, developers and corporate farms draining wetlands and converting forested lands into non-forested landscapes, and you have a displaced population of animals that need somewhere to live.

11

LARGE AND SMALL ANIMAL CONFLICTS

Conflicts with Large Animals

What to look for:
> When the ears of a large animal drop or fold back
> When a large "buck" or "bull" extends his head and neck
> and stares at you
> When body hair seems to bristle, stand up along its back
> When the male tucks his head and advances a few steps

What a large animal might do to you:
> Butt you with its head
> Gore you with its horns or antlers
> Bite you (especially if it is a carnivore intending to kill
> and eat you)

Carnivores prefer out-of-shape prey—more marbling in the meat—so if you are like most Americans, hit the Stairmaster before going outdoors. The odds are small a large animal will kill you, unless you go outside.

How Do You Know When You Are Going To Die from a Large Animal Conflict?

When you are eye-to-eye with pupils larger than yours—unfocused pupils, blood-red pupils above a snot storm blowing from enlarged nostrils, above mouth slobber dripping from loose lips that may or may not pass through the microfleece holes in your Gore-Tex adventure suit.

Conflicts with Small Animals

What to look out for:
> Smaller versions of the previous, often accompanied by
> sharp pains in your legs

What a small animal may do to you:
> Bite you
> Scratch you
> Embarrass your guests by doing their business where
> they have no business being

Small animal bites are very common, but most from "friendly" canines. More than a million Americans seek medical care each year from dog bites, and children—particularly boys five to ten years old—are most often the victims since uniformed employees have gone postal. To put a stop to this, bite the animal back, hard. Human saliva has a much higher bacterial count.

Cats are notorious scratchers and transmit cat-scratch fever along with rabies and toxoplasmosis, which if a pregnant woman is infected within the first trimester can cause abortion. To put a stop to this, de-claw the cats. If that doesn't work, remove their front legs. If that doesn't work, remove their back legs and use the body to block drafts coming under the door.

Domestic dogs and pets show their displeasure by inappropriate behavior. To put a stop to this, show your displeasure by inappropriate behavior (you know what I mean) in their "house."

There is no reason to have a conflict with an animal that is smaller than you. None. Not since man invented the Louisville Slugger, Joe DiMaggio model.

Even Herbivores Can Kill

Zoonoses are diseases that animals pass on to humans—either through direct contact with skin and fluids or indirectly through insects, mites, and ticks that feed on diseased animals. Parasitic diseases include rabies, hantavirus, plague, leptospirosis, brucellosis, salmonellosis, histoplasmosis, trichinosis, and tularemia. Ticks can pass, among others, Rocky Mountain Spotted Fever and Lyme's disease. Combinations of the above deliver fever, chills, shakes, rash, vomiting, diarrhea, convulsions, abdominal pain, and passing into the ethers. Certain diseases such as Black Death are fairly rare, but if the main carrier is a rodent and you are surrounded by a rash of rodents, as in *Willard* (1971), the chances of catching the bubonic plague are higher than normal. Bats are a fairly typical carrier of rabies and while death caused by rabies total less than twenty a year, unconfirmed reports indicate most of these are rabid fans of Anne Rice's vampire novels.

THE MOST UNWANTED ANIMALS

Urban

Number one is raccoons followed by, in no particular order and varied according to part of the country, armadillos, pigeons, bats, cockroaches, birds (crows, pigeons, and grackles), squirrels, opossum, waterfowl (ducks and geese), and rodents. In Chicago, raccoon complaints are twice that for squirrels. In Texas, the armadillo competes with raccoons and illegals for top honors, especially when digging for grubs  in freshly watered lawns during a drought. In Seattle, the mole is number one; the rainwater that gives their coffee such a robust taste and texture pushes up slugs and insects for easy subsurface feeding.

Suburban

Number one is whitetail deer followed by raccoons, woodpeckers, squirrels, beaver, coyote, snakes (nonpoisonous), opossum, waterfowl (ducks and geese), bats, and skunks. Any herbivore appreciates the boomer fixation on gardening and small-plot horticulture.

Rural

Number one is whitetail deer, followed in no particular order by feral pigs, elk, coyotes, beavers, rodents, feral dogs, poisonous snakes, wolves, and skunks. The meat hog is a contender for those who live downwind of the large corporate pig farms.

PHYSICAL ADAPTATIONS TO THE NEW MILLENNIUM

The evolution process of animals is best thought in terms not of just one hundred years, but more appropriately in a thousand-year span. Many of the adaptations discussed below we will not personally witness. They are a legacy to our children and for many of our children, they will have preferred the Acura. Some physical adaptations are impossible. Large animals cannot adapt to a pinched urban environment. Large animals cannot even think small, or eventually shrink unless wildlife geneticists start breeding them for small urban habitats—such as the better rent-control apartments. Small animals sense this vacuum and start thinking large; this inappropriate behavior creates the nuisance wildlife control operator. It's the Great Circle of Life.

Senses

Hearing: Larger ears that can be angled or cocked will be an asset in the noisy city. In the wild, moose are living longer, but exposure to increased traffic noise in national parks has caused their antlers to cup to enhance their hearing capabilities. Fortunately, when antlers fall off, visitor traffic has switched over to the much noisier snowmobile.

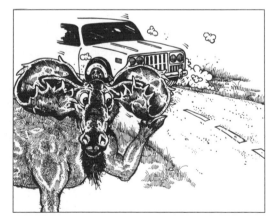

Sight: Grizzlies are very nearsighted, but there is still no need for sight to equal smell when interacting with shortsighted vacationers. Rodents are successful in the city partially due to their ability to see the big picture. Eyes on the side of the head rather than in the middle of a flat face will become an important physical feature for urban survival.

Smell: Garbage heated by city activity is appealing to all newcomers. Asphalt and steel hold the sun's heat, increasing the circulation of aromatic molecules—a theory that makes scents until animals lose their superior sense of smell due to urban pollutants, which is a certainty. City managers now use a measure of five air pollutants to determine if it's safe for citizens to just go outside. Wild animals that move to the city must be concerned with the toxic mix of lead, carbon monoxide, ozone, nitrogen dioxide, sulfur dioxide, and particulate matter in the new environment. Benzene, formaldehyde, and butadiene produced from car emissions alone are enough to cause urban growths that require radiation and chemotherapy. With air pollution in some cities exceeding 400 on a combined scale of 1 to 500, animals might as well take up the habit and smoke unfiltered Camels. Add secondhand smoke from the furtive addicts on break in building alcoves throughout any city and wild animals might as well live in the zoo.

Taste: Carnivores in the wild have their favorite foodstuffs, still it's hard to know if a large cat is guided more by taste than by texture. Most likely gut-wrenching hunger. In the city, carnivores need to be aware of food poisoning. Animals in the wild have a long memory of what's good and not good, yet when they come to the city, the mixed hash of odors and tastes mask real dangers to animal health. In the wild, animals don't need to worry about the growing, inspection, and shipping practices of agribusiness farming the Third World to feed our obsession for fresh fruits and vegetables all year long. In the wild, animals don't need to worry about undercooked hamburger or pork or turkey stuffing or restaurant employees not washing their hands after using the bathroom. Frankly speaking, even the common hot dog could contain listeria. Up and downtown, animals do need to worry about contaminated foods from all sources, in particular from those sources who don't wash their hands after first choking, then not properly refrigerating the chicken. Or the crème puffs or salad dressings. Or eating oysters in the months that don't end in R. For a healthy wild animal, food-borne illnesses may show up as just an upset stomach but for the young, old, and systemically weakened urbanized critters, the gastrointestinal disorders caused by the salmonella group are particularly bothersome: animal diarrhea, prostration, abdominal cramps, nausea, fever, headaches, and projectile vomiting, not to mention the mercury,

PCBs, acid rain, and factory farm and feedlot pollutants in the water needed to wash down a tasty piece of garbage. Not to speak of urban heavy metals, music to few ears. Urban water supplies are threatened by the human population growth and soon the only urban water not politically charged will be baptismal. Herbivores don't have as sophisticated a palate and need not worry as much, but carnivores and omnivores will have to take it easy in their new digs for the first several days.

Touch: The urban metro systems—subways and buses—are where city dwellers touch inappropriately, and it's in the city where "nature" is merchandised to the soft touches long removed from the land. Wild animals that tilt toward domestication will prosper in the land of those touched in the head.

The Sixth Sense: A sense of danger in the wild is dulled in the seemingly friendly suburbs and rubbed raw in the dangerous inner city. The most important other sense in the city is that of humor.

Physical Characteristics

Size: In the wild, male mammals are often larger than the females just because. In the matriarchal city, a better excuse will be needed. The largest mammals are the most resistant to change in habitat and know that if they were to make the in-bound migration, most advantages of size disappear. In the small world, species size makes quite a difference; since raccoons are twice the size of opossums, this makes them first at the pet food dish. An eight-foot, two-inch Big Bird has top billing and cooing in the 'hood. Outside town, the biggest and ugliest birds are on the updraft—turkey vultures, cormorants, and, with a twenty-million-dollar nest egg, the California condor—birds of a feather perched high above the feral cat population.

The size of certain animal body parts has an urban dimension as well. If wild drakes mimicked city males, ducks would mate only with large-breasted hens and the selection process would, unfortunately, produce heavy-breasted birds for the attention and roasting ovens of duck hunters.

Shape: Mammals in the city take on a more amorphous shape. Role models for small children are often large and featureless, like big dummies in feet-in, zip-up pajamas. Many New Yorkers learned their animals as they floated down Broadway on Thanksgiving Day, and to this day are puzzled by the lack of tethers on large park animals.

Head: In an urban environment, the head of an owl must be able to rotate that extra ninety degrees to survive. It also seems that head and face size has a commercial quality in urban culture. Naturalist Stephen Jay Gould has tracked the changes in size of Mickey Mouse's head. As Mickey's character warmed, his head size increased relative to his body size for a more childlike appearance. Perhaps in the future, animals with the larger heads will have the greatest appeal. The Bullwinkle J. Moose estate will be delighted.

Legs: The city is a concrete jungle, and cubs, calves, fawns, and kits are most vulnerable to musculo-skeletal injuries. Growth plate injuries on an immature and growing skeleton are more common in a hardened city where there is no leisurely wake-up call and stretching. Whether injuries are caused by direct impacts from a fall, collision, or simply running on concrete with worn-out pads, the contact produces sore shoulders, heels, and knees. And shin splints. The unusual running, jumping, and turning that characterizes normal urban survival can also cause acute tendonitis. Young mammals and the chicken trying to cross the road suffer from strained hamstrings and sprained ankles caused by manmade implements with hard angles not found in nature.

Paws and Claws: The pads of canines, cats, and bears will harden, and the hoofs of deer and other ungulates will wear and crack like a workman's fingernail unless they stay on the grass. Cat's retractable claws will stay sharp.

Teeth: Teeth used to rip flesh will sharpen to get through the heftier garbage bags and teeth used to chew will need caps once they grind aluminum cans for the first time. The opossum, the animal kingdom's most successful foodaholic, has the largest number of teeth (fifty), but has a hard time holding on to all of them because of interactions with Goodyear and Uniroyal representatives.

Beaks: Bird beaks will toughen as they are schooled in the hard knocks.

Whiskers: The close shaves common to an urban lifestyle will take its toll on animal personal grooming.

Hide: The islands of urban heat will have two major influences on an animal's skin. One is thickness: there is no room for thin-skinned animals in the big city. If a large animal can't stand the heat, it should get the heck out of Hell's Kitchen (now known as Clinton, which has a prosecutorial heat of its own). The other is hair or fur: most mammals have fur with protective guard hairs covering a soft undergrowth or wool hair. If an animal bounces between the hot city and its cooler surroundings, it won't know whether to shed or go blind. There will be less need to have a winter coat; given city people's attitude toward winter fur garments, this is probably a good idea. Camouflage for the young animal, especially whitetail deer, will remain good public relations. The patterns of camouflage may change from soft ovals to sharp rectangles and squares. Spots on this new background will resemble door knobs. The color of a mature coat will eventually soften into an urban gray, a very fashionable platinum from the pollutants in the air. In the sooty industrial cities of the Northeast, the black squirrel and black duck will be joined by blackened color variations of all native animals. Reintroduced carnivores such as the Mexican gray wolf already prefer to look like most anything else—a ground squirrel, a California condor. Anything other than a sheep predator.

Except for tree rodents teetering along a power line, long mammal tails used for balance, protection, and swimming in the wild have little value in the city. A long tail is too easy to grab in the short distances, especially on the east-west blocks of Manhattan. The more sensitive animals would feel clumsy with a long bushy tail that's likely to knock valuable urban things over, whatever valuable urban things are. Hairless tails are repugnant to most humans and other mammals. The flat tail of the beaver is properly used to slap those who say animals can't build something enduring.

Armor: Armadillos are their own armored personnel carriers. Snapping turtles can also take care of themselves.

Quills: Wild porcupines are not interested in what city planners call trees.

Poisons: If the origin of the dance, the tarantella, is from the bite of the tarantula, and the mambo comes from the bite of the mamba snake, who knows what the byte of the twenty-first century will create? With the animals we are shaping, it won't be a simple turkey trot—it'll be more like a jitterbug.

23

Protective scents: Defense sprays such as those used by skunks will intensify in toxicity to compete in the olfactory assault of a large city. A summer garbage strike in any major city would put any skunk to shame.

Life Expectancy

Larger animals live longer because we need them to. What would happen if Mom and Dad bought Missy a pony and just as the bills for the riding lessons came due, the horse just ups and dies? You can bet that would be a horse of another color! Everything is difficult for the big guys—later sexual maturity, longer gestation periods, smaller litters, and longer child rearing—and all are difficult in an urban environment. Mice, on the other paw, die young but party hard, producing large and genetically healthier families during that short life. Smaller animals thrive in smaller places—urban places predisposed to rollover to the pet culture.

Animals that fall under the care and protection of pet or zoo ownership tip life scales. Pigeons in captivity can live fifteen years; in the city park, maybe three to four years on the outside. A golden eagle can live an additional fifteen years in captivity, especially if it has a chance to eat a few of the pigeons next door. Canadian wolves planted into Yellowstone are expected to live long enough to retire with a full federal pension and coyote pup (or black-footed ferret) ration. Life expectancy for human newborns has increased as well, from forty-seven years in 1900 to seventy-five years today. Maximum life span for humans is around 115 years; many of the oldest credit long life to good cigars and the occasional shot of bourbon. Not one credits their spouse.

Fish don't live long because of all the Elks Club tournament fish fries. Occasionally an odd couple catches the oldest catfish in the lake but a three- to five-year-old fish, as measured by the growth rings on the otolith (a bone in the ear spine or fin), is an old timer. Insects don't live long either, which is a good thing.

In the wild, animals quietly retire to the deep, dark woods. There are no such retirement homes in the city. Urban dwellers rely on life-support machines, another reason that animals shouldn't come to town.

ADAPTIVE BEHAVIOR THAT MAY ALLOW WILDLIFE TO SURVIVE

In *On The Origin of Species,* Charles Darwin noted that nature is a "turbulent, dynamic engine of adaptation." In simplest terms, animals in the wild have familiar behaviors and experiences. They eat, woo and mate, have children, lose position to habitat downsizing and ambitious youngsters, and then die. Animals in the wild that are not disturbed by human activities are purebreds, and purebred animals have the most predictable wild behavior. Wild horses act like wild horses, giving rise to sayings like, "fast and erratic doesn't win the race," used mostly when a two-year-old gelding slams into the guard rail from a drug overdose. Hybrid animals—like wolf mixes and the hybrids that own them—have even less predictable behavior. If your wolf/German shepherd mix rearranges the neighbor's features, it's difficult to tell which of the two canine strains is responsible for the inappropriate behavior. The behavior may be one of those left brain-right brain conflicts that can only be corrected with a Louisville Slugger, Joe DiMaggio model.

Animal behavior is learned from mimicking parents and other members of the same species. The exception is behavior altered by an illness such as rabies or other life-threatening diseases. Animals moving to or meeting the city will mimic urban animals and adapt behaviors with a much more human history to survive and thrive.

Hunting and Eating

In the city, an urban animal goes for the kill by circling the dark object in the alley, and going for the neck of the Hefty bag before ripping open the belly of the beast. Coyotes, foxes, and mountain lions concentrate on the viscera. Bears are naturally disappointed in how thin the meat is. Crows are just glad to be invited to the party.

In the wild, carnivores will move about all day long, and herbivores prefer to feed during the gray shoulder periods. These routines are interrupted only during hunting seasons. In the city, feeding necessarily follows human activity; garbage in, garbage out. Great white sharks feed without schedule; they have found that vacationing humans in black wet suits are more difficult to chew and don't taste as good as a similar-looking seal or whale pup, but they have high hopes for the younger, plumper Cousteau.

Animals like otters and gulls that use tools to eat, breaking shells on a rock or dropping clams on a pavement, will prosper in cities full of the gadget-crazy.

Courtship and Mating

Over 95 percent of all mammals are nonmonogamous. Few species mate for life, except high church elders and senior Republicans making their bones on the judiciary committee. Politicians make the mistake of higher primates like the mountain gorilla, who think their biological drives produce the best possible children. Females seeking to produce superior offspring make an even bigger mistake when they go below the belt line inside the Belt Line. Irregular and same-sex encounters are outed by the religious Telly Tubbies.

Birds are a slightly different story. The faithfulness of Canadian geese is well-documented, but biologists note that even honkers waddle astray should the first nesting be unsuccessful. It's hard to imagine songbirds sleeping around, though even chickadees engage in "extra-pair copulations." They're not as bird-brained as originally thought.

Breeding

Rough sex will continue to be a part of a wild mammal's life. For example, the best way to tell a male from a female sea otter is the bite marks on her nose; if you've ever heard cougars or young Italians making love, your first impulse is to dial 911. Swedes will continue to make love in the back seat of Volvo sedans, as it is only there they feel truly safe; Swedish women prefer the station wagon for the "big icky" as the longer bed is less likely to wrinkle their traditional costume; Swedish men prefer Norwegian women, like those robust farm girls from up-fjord. Large cats, bears, and bats all bite the back of the neck of their paramour during copulation, a "get-a-grip" behavior that won't be out of place in the big city.

Growing Up

Cities are awful places for the larger mammals to raise their young. Youngsters will leave deep family traditions, and sever ties to their wild cousins and a neighborhood of familiar rocks, trees, and streams. They lose superior orientation skills to a false reliance on east/west grids. Since the wisest elders will not relocate to the city, those trying to escape the herd mentality fall prey to fast-talking urban dandies, and, since maturing sexually at a much younger age, to underage pregnancies that result in many fatherless children.

Sleeping

Animals look to make their bed in a safe, protected area. Most urban animals prefer the quiet suburbs or its outer edges for this simple reason. They know it's impossible to get a good night's rest in the inner city, and are confused by the random placement of soft spots provided by the city road departments.

Hibernating large animals prefer a quiet den or cave, ditto for small bats. The grizzlies in Yellowstone National Park are being kept awake by the loudmouth gray wolves, and there will be hell to pay in the spring. With the right conditions, a bear may hibernate for up to two hundred days; abandoned buildings in the city are an option only if you crack a few heads first. Even owls retire to the suburbs to sleep, and there is no reason for a goose to leave a quiet, closed golf course. Ducks in city parks often sleep with one eye open, especially those on the outside of the flock. Researchers note that the corresponding half of the duck's brain shuts down, surprising the red fox who finds suspect the very idea of a duck brain and the need for this research.

Birds that have strong homing instincts and appreciate crowded living will easily find comfortable housing in the high-rise urban environment. Purple martins are already true urbanites—they rely on others to provide housing and quickly take to a tightly packed neighborhood. A bird that winters in Brazil when many of us in northern climates are unable to migrate has nothing to complain about. If the martins drive you cuckoo, let the cat out.

Making Noise

Canines have at least five recognizable noises: a growl, bark, howl, whine, and a whimper. All will be important in the city, especially the whine. In the wild, coyotes are true concert performers, hilltop harmonizers that romance listeners much like the Three Tenors; in the city, coyotes will learn to sing on the run with their mouths full, with a likely crossover in tunes to a more marketable pop-classical fusion.

In the wild, elks bugle and bears woof—even with a mouth full of your hide—as the lesser animals move to town. Wherever they live, whitetail deer grunt; the grunt turns into a bleat if you accidentally bump into one backing out of the driveway. Don't worry. The neighbors won't know a thing once you close the trunk. You'll never get close enough to hear a mule deer grunt. If you are close enough to hear a buffalo grunt, enjoy your last few minutes. Animal sounds in the city will change primarily in pitch to rise above the urban clatter.

Daily Migrations

In Northern winter climates, large animals such as moose, deer, and buffalo appreciate the opened road if it leads to and from feeding areas. They appreciate the paths of last resistance (which developers prefer as well). Snowmobile paths and railroad beds run a close second. Unfortunately they haven't learned to walk on the side of the road facing the traffic, giving city managers and motorists alike migration headaches.

Seasonal Migrations

Native salmon have lost much of their genetic codes that give directions to their original spawning beds. However, the bull salmon hasn't lost his reluctance to ask for directions, a necessary tactic if the sexes are to remain distinct.

Highly Stressed Behavior

Stressed behavior is inappropriate behavior in the animal world, often caused by internal growth issues. Population density in whitetail deer populations is a good example. Fifteen to twenty-five deer per square mile allows each the proper elbow room, but when the numbers reach seventy-five and over, whitetail deer seriously compete for the same resources. The "islands" of urban deer populations that number up to two hundred per square mile can be counted on to perform in less dear ways, along an established model for urban conflict.

WATCHING WILDLIFE OF THE NEW MILLENNIUM

WHAT TO TAKE ON YOUR WILDLIFE WATCH

Clothing

In carnivore country, wear anything *but* leather apparel. Leather reminds the largest meat eaters of a dining decision based on tradition. Also, wear only clothing that can be easily torn off while running. Big buttons—bad. Zippers—okay. Velcro—good.

Seasoned field professionals working in snake-infested areas wear three or four pairs of pants. Three to four inches of oilcloth offers particularly effective snakebite protection. Layering clothing is also a very effective method of temperature control. Three to four inches of oilcloth will also keep your meatloaf sandwiches nice and warm if placed on the inside layer.

Don't wear Puma brand shoes in mountain lion country. A big cat will see you as a smart aleck, as well as lunch. In black bear country, wear shoes that will outrun the other members of your party. In grizzly country, add climbing cleats for an extra note of false security.

Wear a cap or hat in open fields, especially in the early evenings when bats are looking for a flat landing spot. Or when black widow spiders are looking for a nest.

Gear

You'll want to carry a set of binoculars for viewing animals in their native habitat, doing what truly wild animals do all day. A set of 7 X 35 lenses are considered minimum in the field. If you feel the bear is getting too close, turn the binoculars around and the bear will appear to be a safe distance from you and your loved ones.

A camera is also suggested to record your day in the field, especially in grizzly bear country where the last frames of exposed film are added to the coroner's report.

Protection

Many wildlife watchers prefer a multipurpose walking stick and/or cane for minimum protection while in the field. Some sticks come with a sharpened point, which is handy for picking up refuse along the trail, nailing a snake to the ground, or poking a horse unwilling to move off the bridle trail. Conflicts with larger animals require a Louisville Slugger, Joe DiMaggio model, or better yet, a twelve-foot sculling oar for those hard-to-reach animals.

On a family vacation in bear country, anything larger than a .357 magnum will make you feel better, but won't make any difference to the bear. Shooting a federally protected grizzly bear, especially in a national park, is a felony; should you need to use the weapon, assure your brother-in-law it's not personal. Given current marital statistics, in-laws are much easier and cheaper to replace, and jury boxes in good hunting areas are packed with sympathetic married men.

Pepper spray is touted as a replacement to serious gun action. Given erratic wind conditions and general aerosol accuracy, the spray should not be used until the bear is ten feet away. By the time the bear is ten feet away and closing, you might as well spray yourself and hope he doesn't like his human Hunan hot!

First Aid Kit

Several two-feet by two-feet plastic sheets for head and
  sucking chest wounds
One large rifle or pistol cartridge
One each, prosthetic arm and leg (rights for the right-
  handed, lefts for the left-handed)
One large size Attends
One pound or more morphine, any form
One five-gallon pail of plasma
One liter of good wine, something that goes well with
  red meat, your red meat
One cellular phone, both digital and analog
One Palm Pilot for your last e-mail messages

Food

Experienced wildlife watchers don't have to sacrifice mature food habits for a day in the field. There is no need to resort to the latest freeze-dried foods designed for less-sophisticated palates. Brown bears recommend a menu that keeps up your strength and adds marbling at the same time.

Breakfast

Two dozen large eggs, any style
One pound bacon
Two 8-packs Jimmy Dean maple-flavored sausage links
Six Dunkin Donuts Old Fashioned Donuts
One gallon prune juice
One fifth Smirnoff vodka

Lunch

One 16-piece bucket Kentucky Fried Chicken, original
formula, with mashed potatoes, cole slaw, and corn on
the cob
One 6-pack Rainbow Jell-O
One case Budweiser longnecks

Midday Snack

One pound warmed Velveeta, mild Mexican
Two large water crackers, or one 10-inch pizza round
One quart Wild Turkey bourbon
One pint Hot Damn
One box Little Debbie Oatmeal Crème Pies

Dinner

Four 10-ounce boneless prime ribs, medium rare
Four baked Idaho russet potatoes
One pint sour cream
One pound butter
One sprig chives
Five pounds Swiss chard
Six large beets
One fifth Galiano
One quart Dad's root beer
Two spears asparagus
One 8-inch lowfat carrot cake
One quart Ben & Jerry's Chocolate Chip Cookie Dough
ice cream

Field Guides

The Roger Tory Peterson Field Guides are almost as useful as a pocket
edition of the Holy Bible earmarked to the passage that begins, "Yea,
though I walk through the valley of the shadow of death."

Other Paper Goods

In any larger-carnivore-than-you country, your last will and testament should be left at the trailhead or with the park ranger. There is
no need for burial instructions as most carnivores provide those services at no cost to the less immediate family.

THE BEST TIME TO VIEW WILDLIFE

Wildlife is best watched when properly stirred, not shaken. Wildlife not stirred is either sleeping or deceased. Be dead certain the grizzly is sleeping the *Big Sleep* or you'll be the basis for an edgier *Dead Man Walking*. The stir-crazy wildlife of the new millennium will maintain a high state of agitation; for those guided by time management, there are better times to view the modern menagerie.

By Day

Wild animals stir early in the morning, much before the average vacationer unless Dad wants to do at least six hundred miles that day. Wild animals have daily habits that rarely vary—sleeping, eating, drinking, staring off into the distance, blinking, wagging their tails, drinking (but not so much that they have to get up later to go potty), and bedding down for the night. Variations on the above routine can be attributed to the mating instinct raising its ugly head in the fall (hunting season). Depending on the species, all daily activities can be observed in a sixteen-hour period, especially if they live in a zoo or Las Vegas hotel.

By Month

Wildlife interacting with urban dwellers are stirred by an artificial calendar. The most significant months are when homebuilders break new habitat into smaller cul-de-sacs, followed by the most important summer months, July and August, when stirrings for a "nature" experience are imagined.

By Season

Waking animals are not at their photogenic best in the spring, and any smaller critter that interrupts its focus on a square meal may become one. Spring is when wild animals have their young and the best opportunity for those interested in viewing an animal nuclear family and the male animal who put her in "that condition" in the first place.

Large furred animals slow considerably in the heat of summer, and are unnaturally forced to speed up during the peak vacation months. For those trained in physics, large furred animals so cranked up carry a significant coefficient of energized inertia and, for those not trained in CPR, deserve room for extended de-acceleration. Herd animals take jobs in PETA roadside petting parks.

The "rut" or Super Bowl of animal sports stirs wild critters without any outside help. Adult males compete for the best-looking, healthiest females, while the females sort through the thick stack of invitations for males most likely to meet their various needs. Rutting males are identified by thickened necks, darker hair color, and single focus on sex. The instinctual urge to go forth and multiply supremely distracts wild animals but, as the earliest Native Americans learned, when crawling on your belly to photograph some close-up wildlife DO NOT wear the hide of a female buffalo, deer, elk, or moose without first inserting a butt-plug.

In the northern climates some animals just curl up and go to sleep for winter. If you want to see a hibernating bear, poke a long stick in a cave. Don't worry about poking them in the eye; they're sleeping and both eyes are closed.

If you wake a bear during the winter, use the fastest lens setting and film ASA. Other large animals, like deer, "yard up" in snow country to conserve energy and celebrate the festive holiday season. Smaller animals like turtles and frogs hide so well in winter you might as well spear fish. Insects are too thin-skinned for extreme cold and die, so birds that rely on them and summer grain crops fly south. Ducks and geese that don't migrate to warmer climates are not playing by the old waterfowl management rules and deserve an extended hunting season and larger bag limits. Wildlife watchers in the winter should head south to Miami and Phoenix to view snowbirds of a similar feather.

WHAT TO LOOK FOR

Tracks

In the wild, animals leave their tracks in mud, snow, loose sand, and dirt. If they don't want to be tracked, they walk on leaves. In urban and suburban locations, the real messy stuff is covered with grass, decorative landscaping, concrete, and asphalt. Animals of all persuasions are loath to track up the white or off-white carpeting sported by the latest housing developments. Tracks drive the does of the owner's species completely wild.

The only city tracks of note are along Hollywood's Walk of Fame; the only animals that strut along that shiny trail are dogs. Amateur trackers need to look closely at an urban square of dirt to identify an animal track. The larger hoofed animals are easiest to identify, and the larger predators that tip-toe (or drive) leave familiar footprints.

Rubbings

In the late summer and early fall, antlered animals polish the new growth of headgear that makes them look so handsome in the woods. These rubbings can be seen in the wild on small saplings and larger trees. Pieces of the "velvet" or moss-like cover may still be attached to the rub spot. In the city, big males ignore the spindly vegetation most landscape architects call trees and rub their trophy racks against

lamp posts and other city verticals. Unfortunately, the metal construction does not hold the scent associated with a vigorous rub and bucks are forced to turn to scrapes as an alternative.

Scrapes

In the wild, bucks and bulls paw and pee in the dirt, leaving a scent trail that warns possible contenders and invites females to a short-term but deeply caring and intimate relationship. In the city, these scrapes are

37

made in city parks where many other short-term relationships are consummated. After a whiff of other park deposits, many animals prefer to scatter a much more impressive scent package.

Scat/Poop

Urination is hard to locate for even the most seasoned wildlife sniffer. Male mammal urine is found ahead of the rear paws; female number one is found behind or between the rear paws. If a male has had too much to drink, urine can be found *on* his legs and paws. Females are much too sensible to involve themselves in that kind of behavior.

Animal scat has important distinguishing features and each helps the wildlife watcher identify the animal for a life book, for those who give a poop.

Poop size: Generally speaking, the larger the poop, the larger the animal. The more poop, the more full of poop the animal is, and the greater likelihood it votes a straight party ticket. Grizzly bear poop can be quite large, especially if a large human body is passed.

Shape: The tunnel that has no light at the end of it determines the shape of animal poop. The ends are normally tapered so the back door doesn't slam shut and wake the other species in the bushes. If the poop has no shape and is loose, the animal is experiencing the same gastric distress as those racing out the front door of the restaurant. Too much MSG will do that.

Texture: Swallowed animal hair twists and often ties the ends of animal poop together on exit. Protruding pieces of aluminum foil and candy wrappers indicate the animal's proximity to a city park. Peanut shells are a dead giveaway. Macadamia nuts are too expensive for any species to pass.

Color: Crushed bone will give animal poop a dull white appearance. Fruit and berry skins will color accordingly. As famed wildlife biologist Sam Blake knows, a small pile of berry husks may be a sign to bear witness, or more appropriately, arms.

Smell: Animal poop smells as bad as human waste. Domesticated animals eat human poop and when they do, you can't imagine the horror. A grizzly bear's human farts score much higher on the smell-o-meter than a human's kim chee farts. Lighting a grizzly bear fart may be the only sure defense and your Zippo lighter better light in that gale.

Distribution: Much like urine or scent markings, scattered feces are territorial signs. If you see poop in neat little piles, that animal has too much time on its paws and deserves an open season.

Trails

Well-grounded animals leave a trail of activity between where they eat and sleep. In the wild, these trails follow the natural contours of the land and are distinguished by the particular nature of the animal. A wild pig will track through the thickest brush; whitetail deer avoid heavy brush until hunting season. Carnivores leave a very distinct trail of heel marks as they drag your watchdog out to play.

Beds/Nests

In the wild, animals construct simple to elaborate nests in and under trees, and in tree trunks, tall grass, and fallen timber. Bed locations are selected for their relative safety and proximity to food and water. In the city, the best locations are already taken by Nature's Stewards and, since many city parks close at dusk, wild animals compete with other subspecies for shelter.

THE BESTIARY
AMPHIBIANS, BIRDS, FISH, INSECTS, MAMMALS, AND REPTILES

AMPHIBIANS

Salamanders are the first of the three major families of amphibians; now that Newt has slipped out of sight, they are possibly the least important. The second family of limbless burrowers are even less visible to the naked eye.

Frogs and toads are vanishing at an alarming rate, and biologists offer an incomplete list of reasons: ultraviolet light, acid rain, pesticides, toxic fungus, viruses, and/or a gastric aversion to rice-based beer. The thin-skinned amphibians can absorb only so much abuse.

FROG

ALIASES: Minnesota Northern leopard frog, Legs

SCIENTIFIC NAME: *Rana* "The Body" *pipiens*

PERSONAL CHARACTERISTICS: A frog will be anywhere from two to five inches long. Adults with two legs weigh four to six ounces, with each extra leg adding an ounce.

WHERE TO VIEW: General distribution is in the toxic waters of the Land of 10,000 Lakes and many more states. The best place is northwest Minnesota, and the worst place, should toxic conditions spread, is in Calaveras County, California, right around jumping season.

WHEN TO VIEW: The legs are best seen during happy hour at a good French restaurant.

WHAT TO LOOK FOR: Multiple footprints.

TIPS TO INCREASE LIKELIHOOD OF SEEING: Drink a certain kind of beer, lots of a certain kind of beer, you know, made from rice.

OLD DIET: Insects, spiders, worms, and crustaceans.

NEW DIET: Beer, beer nuts, beef jerky, and hard-boiled eggs.

OLD BEHAVIOR: Stage gigs as the frog prince, avoiding gigs elsewhere—especially those that supply Biology 101 labs.

NEW BEHAVIOR: The legs on the advertising bullfrogs outside the lake tavern aren't shown. Why? Because the creative director is eating them with a light butter sauce, that's why.

LIKELIHOOD OF SIGHTING IN THE NEW MILLENNIUM: One hundred percent. Frogs absorb pollutants through their skin and are an early warning sign of a chemical holocaust. Insecticide manufacturers are subsidizing efforts to breed a thicker-skinned frog.

FUTURE: During a long evolution, the frog lost its swimming tail and have recently been in danger of losing their legs to the restaurant industry. In Minnesota and elsewhere, frogs with more than two legs (many akimbo, a favorite Cajun dish) are hopping mad about the new limb abnormalities. The deformities are more often found in frogs that spend their life in water, which led leading Swedish herpetologists to realize legs are part of the frog that is often under water. Hesitant to jump to any conclusions, a Scandinavian task force has been organized to turn the frogs over to see if two heads result.

TOAD

ALIASES: Common American, Mr. Toad

SCIENTIFIC NAME: *Bufo americanus (terrestris)*

PERSONAL CHARACTERISTICS: Toads are a little heftier than frogs, but not much. Adults will measure the same two to five inches long, but bulk up and tip the scales at almost half a pound.

WHERE TO VIEW: General distribution is on a stool, east of a line roughly following the Mississippi River. The best place to see a toad is at http://www.savethetoadplease.com. The worst place is at the Magic Kingdom, where a wild ride long favored by burned-out sixties acidheads is being replaced by some Pooh thing.

WHEN TO VIEW: Night time is the right time.

WHAT TO LOOK FOR: Warts on your body from handling a toad.

TIPS TO INCREASE LIKELIHOOD OF SEEING: Listen for the pleasant trill of the male toad on a warm summer evening.

OLD DIET: Invertebrates.

NEW DIET: Inveterate invertebrates.

OLD BEHAVIOR: The early Christians saw the toad as symbolizing the sin of the filthiest lust. The religious right still sees what they see.

NEW BEHAVIOR: Mr. Toad of *The Wind in the Willows* fame could not be trusted to do what you expected. But toad-like independence is this amphibian's saving grace. "The clever men at Oxford/Know all there is to be knowed/But they none of them know one half as much/As intelligent Mr. Toad." (This was written before our most infamous Rhodes scholar indulged in toad-like behavior in the Oval Office.)

LIKELIHOOD OF SIGHTING IN THE NEW MILLENNIUM: Fifty-fifty.

FUTURE: True toads secrete toxins that irritate the mucous membranes of their predators, giving them two legs up on the more tasty-limbed frogs. Endangered boreal toads irritate the mucous membranes of all ski area development teams. The giant marine toad can irritate the mucous membranes of marine developers from over two feet away. Go toads!

BIRDS

Birds are benefiting from the growth in numbers of serious birders. There are estimated sixty million bird watchers in the United States, many with detailed life books. All this attention is enough to give Tweety an even bigger head. Like Snoopy, this waterhead has sold out to the ad councils.

Birders like pretty birds, pretty birds that talk, whistle, and sing. Birders in the twenty-first century will need a life book specifically for black birds, cowbirds, cormorants, and any other environmental mutants that cackle, caw, and, hopefully, croak.

CROW

ALIASES: American crow, Jim Crow (Old South), common crow, black bird, grackle, Sheryl

SCIENTIFIC NAME: *Corvus brachyrhynchos*

PERSONAL STATISTICS: Adults are nineteen to twenty-two inches long, and weigh about one pound before cooking.

WHERE TO VIEW: General distribution is on top of any dumpster of any shopping mall in America. The best place is on top of the city dump, if it hasn't been paved over for a new housing development.

Black crows are the best Dots chew candy for the movies and are now available in their own box.

Van Gogh's "Crows Over the Wheat Field" is another good place to view crows. The dread expressed by the approaching birds has ominous implications as this painting was his last picture before committing suicide, created after hacking off part of his ear. At least Vincent didn't have to listen to the dreadful riffs of The Black Crowes.

The worst place to view a crow is at any personal reenactment of *The Teachings of Don Juan: A Yaqui Way of Knowledge*.

WHEN TO VIEW: When the garbage trucks bring in the fresh goods.

WHAT TO LOOK FOR: Roadkill and garbage bags ripped open by raccoons and feral pets.

WHAT TO LISTEN FOR: In the Latin liturgy, *Nigra sum sed formosa*.

TIPS TO INCREASE LIKELIHOOD OF SEEING: None needed.

OLD DIET: Any old thing.

NEW DIET: Any new thing.

OLD BEHAVIOR: Making less aggressive birds eat crow.

NEW BEHAVIOR: A flock of these black birds is called a murder of crows, which is just what will come to mind.

LIKELIHOOD OF SIGHTING IN THE NEW MILLENNIUM: One hundred percent. Supermalls hide their garbage well but urban sprawl guarantees a continued supply of strip mall dumpsters.

FUTURE: A true reflection of uncontrolled urban development, the insatiable crow flies the trail of human refuse (sometimes up to fifty miles in one day), snacking at unsanitary landfills on the way to scavenge overflowing dumpsters under the protective twenty-four-hour security lighting of the true heart and soul of urban life—the shopping mall. Over twenty distinct crow calls have been identified and, with each a mystery, you can be sure that the loudest of this diverse shopper is *"¡su basura es mi basura!"*

DUCK (hybrid)

ALIASES: Park duck, sitting duck, shit duck

SCIENTIFIC NAME: *Anas anus*

PERSONAL STATISTICS: An adult will stretch out twenty to twenty-four inches long and weigh two to three pounds, give or take a feather.

WHERE TO VIEW: General distribution is wherever wild mallards have co-mingled with domestic ducks in city parks, green belts, and other soft-focus urban and suburban habitats. It is the best of places to view a duck, it is the worst of places—at the park.

WHEN TO VIEW: Anytime. Park ducks feed all day long.

WHAT TO LOOK FOR: Feathers. Many first-time birders are surprised to learn ducks don't wear sailor suit tops.

TIPS TO INCREASE LIKELIHOOD OF SEEING: Bring a loaf of day-old bread to the park bench. Tear and toss.

OLD DIET: Grains, grass, seeds, and aquatic vegetation.

NEW DIET: Anything that is thrown from the park bench, dry bread.

OLD BEHAVIOR: Sleeping, eating, head bobbing, mating, sleeping.

NEW BEHAVIOR: Mallards were once satisfied with life in the wild, with infrequent dalliances with pintails and gadwalls. Influenced by the looser morals of the inner city, the mallard now engages in inappropriate behavior in the new breeding and nesting areas.

Most duck species have been loathe to cross the species line. (Special Tip: Overweight, trusting, park ducks don't move fast, even for a twelve-year-old with a pocket full of rocks.)

LIKELIHOOD OF SIGHTING IN THE NEW MILLENNIUM: If snapping turtles and the red fox are not reintroduced into city parks, 100 percent.

FUTURE: Ever since Mrs. Mallard led Jack, Kack, Lack, Mack, Nack, Ouack, Pack, and Quack across Boston's Beacon Street in 1941, urban dwellers *Make Way for Ducklings* in their public gardens.

"It certainly isn't what I expected."

SPECIAL DUCK BONUS
Urban Duck Personals

DRAKES SEEKING HENS

LIFE IS SHORT Why not live a little? Juvenile mallard drake seeks older hen for friendship, possible pair-forming, probable treading. x 264

SOUTHERN COMFORT Florida mottled duck seeks black duck hen for discreet liaison. x 717

BASIC INSTINCT Pair-maintaining adult greenhead seeks any hen, any species, any place, anywhere for sensual and mutually rewarding relationship. Confidentiality assured. x 001

VARIETY IS THE SPICE OF LIFE! Coot looking for any "real" duck hen for head bobbing, maybe more. x 231

HENS SEEKING DRAKES

MATURE HEN PINTAIL Seeks stable, mature drake, for swimming around, soft peeping. No dogs. x 429

EUROPEAN HEN WIDGEON Interested in American drake baldpate (not too bald) for friendship, possible pair formation. x 126

TOP GUNS ONLY! Attractive female greater scaup looking for ace who wants to join the Two Thousand Feet Club! No lessers. x 312

DRAKES SEEKING DRAKES

THE CALL OF THE WILD Healthy, full-figured park mallard hybrid scanning the stars for a kindred spirit last heard in the spring heading north. Will go either way. x 691

HENS SEEKING HENS

GREENHEAD HEN Looking for relationship(s), possible support group with other mallard hens tired of drake infidelities. x 969

EAGLE

ALIAS: Bald eagle

SCIENTIFIC NAME: *Haliaeetus leucocephalus,* grade level four

PERSONAL STATISTICS: Adult males hike up to the scales at eight to ten pounds, and the female breaks out at ten to sixteen pounds. They both stretch out from three to three and one-half feet, with six- to eight-foot wingspans.

WHERE TO VIEW: General distribution is rivers and coasts; the mid-Atlantic, Florida, northern Minnesota and Michigan, and the mountainous West. Look for the highest concentrations in Alaska, particularly the Haines-Chilkat Refuge with its large wintering population. The worst place is when building a nest on your undeveloped property.

WHEN TO VIEW: On a perch in the early morning, soaring mid-day on warm thermals, and as a group on senior discount waiting for a noon check-in at the Hotel California.

WHAT TO LOOK FOR: Casinos, concert halls, and on the golf course where a birdie is real and a double eagle if you hit the nest.

TIPS TO INCREASE LIKELIHOOD OF SEEING: Go to a numismatic convention but beware: in 1997, the U.S. Mint slipped a platinum coin into its American eagle bullion coin series.

OLD DIET: Fish, more fish, birds, and carrion.

NEW DIET: Anything an osprey has in its talons, and small tourists.

OLD BEHAVIOR: For the ancients, the eagle was the conductor of souls to heaven. More recently, this bird soars until he poops payroll checks for federal employees.

The Steve Miller Band's "Fly Like An Eagle" is used by the U.S. Postal Service. It should be noted

49

that Federal Express and UPS are not such dodos, using a fish-stealing bird as a symbol of delivery.

NEW BEHAVIOR: In the workplace, it's difficult to soar with eagles when you work with a bunch of turkeys, especially in the government sector. The census bureau may use sharp-eyed eagles to locate missing persons.

LIKELIHOOD OF SIGHTING IN THE NEW MILLENNIUM: With the number of bald eagles in the lower forty-eight at ten times higher than their lowest point in 1963 (over four thousand breeding pairs), the odds of sighting a fully mature, truly bald eagle are good. However, the likelihood of sighting our national emblem with tail feathers intact near a Native American ceremonial plucking center remains remote.

FUTURE: Bald eagles have made a remarkable recovery since the days of heavy use of DDT, which affected egg growth. Now with the use of that chemical banned in the United States, the eggs are hard, healthy, and it takes only two to make a good omelet.

FALCON (Peregrine)

ALIASES: Duck hawk, great footed hawk (Audubon), "Death From Above" (all slower flying birds)

SCIENTIFIC NAME: *Falco peregrinus*

PERSONAL STATISTICS: You don't want to know an adult's dead weight. It's a felony. This bird does average to be fifteen to twenty inches long. Typical of many raptors, females are slightly larger than males.

WHERE TO VIEW: General distribution is most any habitat, more likely along both coasts, and on the edge or ledge of your urban existence. The best place to catch a peek is on the bridges and buildings of Chicago, New York City, Seattle, and other Gothams. The worst place is near your prized pigeon coop. With just the shadow of an airborne peregrine, your favorite will be a stool-less pigeon—no lie!

WHEN TO VIEW: When office workers take a break.

WHAT TO LOOK FOR: Park pigeon feathers, birds engaged in elaborate evasive aerial behavior.

TIPS TO INCREASE LIKELIHOOD OF SEEING: Hold a park pigeon in your hand or over your head, while in any city park.

OLD DIET: Primarily wild birds (except the spine-tailed swift) taken in flight. In the wild, with a diving speed of 175 mph, this bird of prey leaves a slower flying bird without a prayer.

NEW DIET: Primarily feral/domestic birds in flight and at rest. To "do lunch" in the big city, this raptor need only follow the breadcrumbs thrown from a park bench for a no-squabble squab.

OLD BEHAVIOR: Nesting in cliffs and other high locations that offer protection and thermal updrafts near food sources; trying to get over the embarrassment of Ford Motor's slow-moving, late fifties namesake response to the Volkswagen and other imports.

NEW BEHAVIOR: Like the Maltese falcon, always showing up when you least expect them by nesting in surrogate cliffs—ledges on skyscrapers high above city parks full of pigeons.

NEW OCCUPATION IN THE NEW MILLENNIUM: Hired assassin for swarming birds over JFK and other major metropolitan airport runways.

LIKELIHOOD OF SIGHTING IN THE NEW MILLENNIUM: One hundred percent. There are over sixteen hundred breeding pairs in the United States.

FUTURE: Our perception of wilderness has changed so much that we consider it normal that peregrine falcons choose tall buildings in large cities as their homes. Of all the raptors, the falcon feels most comfortable near the tall housing of humans. Nesting on ledges high above and amid the noisy nests of members of the National Audubon Society, these hunters struggle to maintain their keen hunting skills and predator culture in a land of gatherers. The recent exposure to office buildings and, more importantly, office workers are the greatest threats to the rarely imitative raptors.

GOOSE (giant)

ALIASES: Canadian honker, sky carp, tundra maggot (lesser)

SCIENTIFIC NAME: *Branta canadensis maxima*

PERSONAL STATISTICS: An average adult stuffed with a serious amount of goose doo will weigh up to thirteen pounds average (this same adult can drop up to one pound of doo a day). Stretched out, the goose will measure twenty-two to forty inches long.

WHERE TO VIEW: General distribution is over and on any golf course. The best place is in the movie *Fly Away Home* (1996), or in Canada, where their citizenship papers are valid. The worst place is in the above movie, or on your private membership golf course.

WHEN TO VIEW: At tee-off time.

WHAT TO LOOK FOR: Scat, everywhere. Like high-priced athletes, they just DOO it! Also on the sixth day of Christmas, when any self-respecting true love hands out six geese a-laying.

TIPS TO INCREASE LIKELIHOOD OF SEEING: Play golf.

TIPS TO DECREASE LIKELIHOOD OF SEEING: Double up on the use of the pesticide diazinon.

OLD DIET: Plants high in protein, assorted grains, grasses, and aquatic vegetation.

NEW DIET: Any properly mowed and fertilized grass, especially Kentucky blue grass and other succulents found on the fairways and aprons of golf course greens.

OLD BEHAVIOR: Like cranes and ducks, geese don't have homing instincts and must be learned from adults. Imprinting, a technique developed by the Austrian ethnologist Konrad Lorenz in the 1930s, taught greylag geese to bond, sometimes with Konrad, a lot of times with the carpet in his study.

NEW BEHAVIOR: Canada geese used to mate for life in their second or third year. Urban geese will find another mate should their first lovebird fall out of the sky, and in the new century, may imitate the infidelities of the other bird brains in the park. They will also become active in petitioning golf course managers to initiate predator control programs for egg-sucking raccoons.

LIKELIHOOD OF SIGHTING IN NEW MILLENNIUM: Excellent.

LIKELIHOOD OF GOING ON A WILD GOOSE CHASE IN THE NEW MILLENNIUM: One hundred percent.

FUTURE: A giant subspecies, once thought to be extinct, was discovered near Rochester, Minnesota, and have so successfully recovered on a diet of golf-course grasses that they want to join the PGA as non-dues paying members. The "new" goose waddles on plastic cleated webbed feet; with its bad memory, it will put a great amount of effort into hatching range balls in the rough.

Attention Golfers! If your golf ball accidentally "lodges" in a Canadian Goose, you can, without penalty, place another ball near the place where the big dumb bird was when the "lodging" occurred.

ALIASES: Seagull, silverback, silvery gull

SCIENTIFIC NAME: *Larus argentus*

PERSONAL STATISTICS: The breasts of a large gull weigh about two ounces. Bread and fry until golden brown. The length of an adult is eleven to thirty inches.

WHERE TO VIEW: General distribution is behind fishing boats and on the outside decks of any fish and chips restaurant on both coasts of the United States. The best places are in the San Diego Sports Arena and that old Hitchcock movie. Not the one with Kim Novak, the other one. The worst place is in Richard Bach's oxygen-deprived *Jonathan Livingston Seagull.*

WHEN TO VIEW: Before they get to the fries in the fish and chips basket.

WHAT TO LOOK FOR: White-streaked buildings, streets, cars, and people.

TIPS TO INCREASE LIKELIHOOD OF SEEING: Get the big order of fries.

OLD DIET: Coastal garbage, dead marine life, and tern eggs.

NEW DIET: Coastal garbage, flotsam, jetsam, migrating warblers, and debris.

OLD BEHAVIOR: The smaller California gull has its own monument in Salt Lake City, dedicated to those selfless birds who ate the locusts eating the first crops of the Mormon pioneers. City fathers pray for another Miracle of the Gulls to rid the city of the lotus-eaters profiting from the Winter Olympics.

NEW BEHAVIOR: Less gullible and taking more risks. Along the California coast, female gulls are pairing off under the cover of identical gender color and markings.

LIKELIHOOD OF SIGHTING IN THE NEW MILLENNIUM: One hundred percent, no problem.

FUTURE: The herring gull is a tool-user, dropping clam shells on the windshields of those who don't share their snacks. Seagulls are so ubiquitous they're thought of in some bird-brained circles as eco-birds, picking up human garbage on the beach. Any animal that relies on human garbage will live to a ripe, ripe old age.

OWL

ALIASES: Woodsy, hooter, screech owl, tawny owl

SCIENTIFIC NAME: *Otus asio*

PERSONAL STATISTICS: Adults weigh two to two and one-half pounds and stand ten inches tall.

WHERE TO VIEW: General distribution is open woods, suburbs, and small towns. The best place is at any of the fine Hooters restaurants around the country, but beware: Hooters gals attract the Great Horned Owl (*Bubo bubba*). The worst place is in your chimney.

WHEN TO VIEW: Only at night.

WHAT TO LOOK FOR: Owl fur balls.

WHAT TO LISTEN FOR: The screech when they stand too close to the microphones.

TIPS TO INCREASE LIKELIHOOD OF SIGHTING: Imitate mouse sounds or call.

OLD DIET: Rodents and insects.

NEW DIET: Pet rodents and insects.

OLD BEHAVIOR: Acting as a wise old owl. The hearing of the owl is very acute. Dr. Dolittle's owl Too-Too claimed to be able to tell, "using only one ear, the color of a kitten from the way it winks in the dark."

NEW BEHAVIOR: Getting very owlish as spokes-bird losing the battle in the anti-pollution public relations program for the U.S. Forest Service. Given the lyrics it has to sing, "Give A Hoot, Don't Pollute," it's no wonder. A truly wise old owl knows the importance of good lyrics in our postmodern pop culture.

LIKELIHOOD OF SIGHTING IN THE NEW MILLENNIUM: One hundred percent.

FUTURE: The media spotlight almost blinded these reclusive and gentle denizens of the dark during the congressional flim-flam on the reauthorization of the Endangered Species Act. Spotted owls finally realized the unwitting role they played in reforming public opinion on logging practices and now encourage their landlords to bone up on property rights and vote Republican. The pecking order in the federally micro- and mis-managed owl habitat is askew and nobody seems to give a hoot.

PIGEON (feral)

ALIASES: Rock dove, Walter, Homer, "rats with wings"

SCIENTIFIC NAME: *Columba livia*

PERSONAL STATISTICS: Adults weigh up to a pound and stretch from ten to fourteen inches. If you have someone holding their feet tight, they can be stretched even further.

WHERE TO VIEW: General distribution is throughout the great

urban canyons of the United States. The best places are buildings where openings allow space for roosting, loafing, and nest building; churches with ornate architectural features are a prime location. The worst place is directly under them.

WHEN TO VIEW: Before they start their bombing runs.

WHAT TO LOOK FOR: Loose bowel markings on urban statues of forgotten generals and buildings.

TIPS TO INCREASE LIKELIHOOD OF SEEING: Stand outside church in a dark suit, your good one.

OLD DIET: Pigeons have few taste buds so everything tastes sort of good to them. Primarily seed eaters.

NEW DIET: Any stale old bread thrown from a park bench before that damn duck gets it.

OLD BEHAVIOR: Carrying messages of war and sport, pouting.

NEW BEHAVIOR: Replacing the dove by trying with great difficulty to carry olive branch, symbol of peace.

LIKELIHOOD OF SIGHTING IN THE NEW MILLENNIUM: One hundred percent.

FUTURE: For the carrier pigeon, limited. The passenger pigeon passed quietly in the night, something this city bird refuses. Doesn't like to be pigeonholed, or squab introduced to the menu. Likes the use of clay pigeons on the gun range. Doesn't volunteer to be a stool pigeon unless enrolled in the Federal Witness Protection Program.

SONGBIRD

ALIASES: Tweety, et al.

VARIETIES: Canaries, goldfinches, cardinals, bluebirds, orioles, mourning doves, nuthatches, and chickadees. If you put your ear real close to the mouth of a hummingbird, you'll hear the happy humming of your favorite song.

PERSONAL STATISTICS: Adults don't weigh a whole lot, but can pull together enough feathers to be six to twelve inches in length.

WHERE TO VIEW: General distribution is across the United States in or near plants and trees that give shelter and harbor insects.

The best place for viewing a robin is when it comes bob, bob, bobbing along, mostly when neotropical birds migrate through an area. The worst place to view baby songbirds is on the ground, when dislodged by cowbirds and other nest scavengers, and stalked by feral cats. The worst place to hear a songbird is coming out of the business end of Kenny G's saxophone.

WHEN TO VIEW: When your cat coughs up its first hairball of the day.

WHAT TO LOOK FOR: Songbird feathers in your cat's mouth.

TIPS TO INCREASE LIKELIHOOD OF SEEING: Let Sylvester out— he'll never catch Tweety, not if the Commemorative Division of the U.S. Post Office has its say. Their 1998 Tweety and Sylvester stamp series was beat only by the Elvis Presley issue.

TIPS TO DECREASE LIKELIHOOD OF SEEING: Don't feed the feral felines tomcatting about your neighborhood.

OLD DIET: Seed, suet, fruit, nectar, fruit berries, insects, and earthworms.

NEW DIET: Black sunflower seeds, white proso millet, and during the holidays, a nice selection of holiday nuts.

OLD BEHAVIOR: The mockingbird is one of the noisiest songbirds, so much so that Harper Lee published her classic guidebook, *To Kill a Mockingbird,* to put an end to that obnoxious tweeting. Another songbird, the robin, is traditionally the first sign of spring but what with alternating El Niño and La Niñas, that's now a half-cocked notion.

NEW BEHAVIOR: Small birds such as barn swallows will attack cats and rodents in open fields with precision and stealth. Urban songbirds are affected by the urban pollution levels but the major threats, other than losing the habitat on both ends of their migration, are the digital TV and PCS towers necessary to connect bird-lovers to home base. These will knock songbirds for a loop.

LIKELIHOOD OF SIGHTING IN THE NEW MILLENNIUM: Only 99 percent.

FUTURE: On the whole, songbirds are not in as dramatic a decline as reported. Grassland birds (and grasslands) are, as are some forests and forest birds. The bad news is that on the whole, songbird-eating domestic cats are not in dramatic decline. Songbirds are usually too busy singing a happy tune to hear Garfield quietly scaling his way up the pole. Birds that flock together will do best in these troubled times. The songbird of the future may be an occasional whistler, or in feral cat country, a mute, or only a humming-bird, but most certainly a bird with a thickened forehead from crashing into picture windows.

STARLING (European)

ALIASES: Flying cockroach, airborne rat

SCIENTIFIC NAME: *Sturns vulgaris*

PERSONAL STATISTICS: Adults are a prissy two to three ounces and a delicate seven to eight inches long.

WHERE TO FIND: General distribution is everywhere. The best place to find them is Nero Wolfe's table, combined with salt, chervil, basil, thyme, dry sherry, butter, and sage leaves. The absolutely worst place to sight swarming starlings is on take-off. A jet engine stuffed with starling parts will prematurely close your frequent flyer account.

WHEN TO VIEW: In late fall, starlings will group in huge flocks, sometimes hundreds of thousands, and create apocalyptic night-mares for street evangelists and seers.

WHAT TO LOOK FOR: Blackened skies.

TIPS TO INCREASE LIKELIHOOD OF SEEING: Have an apocalyptic point of view.

OLD DIET: Insects, fruit seeds, grain, and grapes.

59

NEW DIET: The better grapes like Pinot Noir and Chardonnay.

OLD BEHAVIOR: Starlings are terrific mimics and imitate all sorts of animal sounds. "Nay, I'll have a starling shall be taught to speak nothing but 'Mortimer.' " William Shakespeare, *Henry IV*.

NEW BEHAVIOR: Starlings kill martins and other small songbirds for their nest, especially a rent-controlled nest.

LIKELIHOOD OF SIGHTING IN THE NEW MILLENNIUM: One hundred percent.

FUTURE: These obnoxious birds are on the Audubon hit list—where they belong.

TURKEY (Wild)

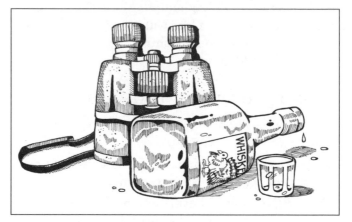

ALIASES: Old Tom, Gobbler, Hedda Gobbler (Norwegian female), Uncle Tom (Old South)

SCIENTIFIC NAME: *Meleagris gallopavo*

PERSONAL STATISTICS: Adults weigh fifteen to twenty pounds and are thirty-six to forty-five inches long.

WHERE TO VIEW: General distribution is in every state but Alaska, behind every office door with a nameplate reading "Boss." The best place is on the label of an empty quart bottle, and on the *South Park* Thanksgiving Special where crazed turkeys poked out everyone's eyes. The worst place is on the label of a quart bottle, and in Turkey where wild "birds" have no civil rights.

WHEN TO VIEW: During mating season.

WHAT TO LOOK FOR: Tracks, feathers, quaking from raw sucking fear during holiday seasons . . . figure it out.

TIPS TO INCREASE LIKELIHOOD OF SEEING: Bowl three consecutive strikes.

OLD DIET: Acorns, berries, seeds, insects, and small reptiles.

NEW DIET: Acorns, berries, more seeds, less insects, and small reptiles only on special occasions.

OLD BEHAVIOR: Turkey trotting, going cold turkey, and talking turkey until it's all so much gobbledygook, just like Benjamin Franklin who wanted the wild turkey to be the national bird.

NEW BEHAVIOR: Disdain for domestic cousins willing to participate in frozen turkey bowling at the local supermarket.

LIKELIHOOD OF SIGHTING IN THE NEW MILLENNIUM: Excellent, 100 percent, couldn't be better.

FUTURE: Beards and primitive feathers that grow at the middle of the breast are usually found on the male turkey, but a female may grow a beard too. In the unisex new century, it's expected that more hens will grow beards and become more difficult to beard.

WOODPECKER

ALIASES: Pileated woodpecker, Woody

SCIENTIFIC NAME: *Dryocopus pileatus*

PERSONAL STATISTICS: The adult is a lightweight, and measures up to twenty inches long, including pecker.

WHERE TO VIEW: General distribution with the hairy woodpecker is out on the fringes of the suburbs, eastern United States, and the Pacific Northwest. The best place is back in the woods where they belong. The worst place is on the side of your house.

WHEN TO VIEW: When their bill comes through your drywall.

WHAT TO LOOK FOR: Holes in your wood siding or yard poles, a true redhead.

WHAT TO LISTEN FOR: Rat-tat-tat.

TIPS TO INCREASE LIKELIHOOD OF SEEING: Build with cedar shakes.

OLD DIET: Insects, tree sap, inner tree bark and, like the common flicker, an ant or two for a quick pick-me-up.

NEW DIET: Wood siding.

OLD BEHAVIOR: Known for being able to cling to tree trunks and punch holes to spear trapped insects with their long, hard tongue. Downed tree trunks, too. Or power line poles, freshly covered with creosote or not.

NEW BEHAVIOR: Clinging to the side of your house and punching holes through your wood siding for insects and to build a nest. To stop this inappropriate behavior, nail a piece of sheet metal over popular pecking area and cover with woodprint drawer-liner paper. The dead sound will also not act as a drumming ground for an amorous male.

LIKELIHOOD OF SIGHTING IN THE NEW MILLENNIUM: One hundred percent.

FUTURE: The large ivory-billed woodpecker found in the south central/east United States is on the endangered species list due to the illicit scrimshaw trade. The other species will survive and thrive; woodpeckers are the only birds that really know how to use its head. Any animal that beats its head against the wall has a chance to be a national emblem in the new millennium.

FISH

The health of our national marine fisheries is a fine kettle of fish. Resource managers apparently have other fish to fry. Commercial overfishing off both coasts has strip-mined seemingly inexhaustible supplies of codfish and pollock. The partisan politics governing salt-water fisheries guarantees no long view. Calling commercial salt-water fishing "harvesting" disguises the fact that these "harvesters" put nothing back—no seed stock, nothing. Stinking from the head, corporate fish management are on the take and when the take disappears, they blame everyone else. The sport fishermen. The Canadians. The Indians. Science. So the smoke screen is to raise hatchery fish to replace the saltwater fish that used to migrate upriver where voters live and quietly invest in fish farms.

The oceans are too large for our pollution, even with cruise boats dumping condoms and other tourist detritus overboard. This is not to say large waters are forgiving. Habitat destruction on or near rivers is enormous.

Accidentally introduced species, such as goldfish from college dorms growing to immense sizes in the Charles River, often fare better than native stock, much to the disadvantage of more polite locals. Some species actually excel in polluted urban waters and artificial waterways that create expensive real-estate frontage, yet few anglers pursue much less eat the radioactive three-eyed fish.

Fish, the first vertebrates, have over forty thousand known species. It's unlikely many will see jawless fish like the lamprey but it is likely that everyone, the almost fifty million that enjoy fishing, will see the following three in their recreational pursuits.

CATCH-AND-RELEASE FISH

ALIAS: Rainbow trout

SCIENTIFIC NAME: *Salmo giardneri*

PERSONAL STATISTICS: Will weigh up to forty pounds and be up to three feet long.

WHERE TO VIEW: General distribution is within a false cast of any Orvis shop or approved lodge, and urban males flyfishing through a midlife crisis. The best place is the Madison River, the South Platte River, the Yellowstone River and in Norman

Maclean's *A River Runs Through It*. The worst place is Robert Redford's *A River Runs Through It* (1993), or anywhere else fly-fishermen have their fly down.

WHEN TO VIEW: During the false hatch.

WHAT TO LOOK FOR: On shore, look for Land Rovers, barn jackets, wicker picnic baskets, Cabernet-Merlot wine blends, and warmed Brie and walnuts. On the fish, look for net burns.

TIPS TO INCREASE LIKELIHOOD OF SEEING: Fuss with your flies until it's dark.

OLD DIET: Insects, in all their forms.

NEW DIET: Artificial nymphs, dry and wet flies.

OLD BEHAVIOR: Native rainbows fight, look, and taste better than other trout. A wild rainbow outside the hallowed honey holes of the flyfishing elite is a marine marvel.

NEW BEHAVIOR: Codependent on the survival and growth of fly-fishing. A plump cutthroat or brook trout in a Montana spring creek has been caught, kissed, and released so many times that fly fishermen should be sued for alienation of affection during off-season. Even trout fry tire of this seasonal exercise and at some point yearn only for a swim in garlic butter.

LIKELIHOOD OF SIGHTING IN THE NEW MILLENNIUM: Ninety-nine percent or less.

FUTURE: The catch-and-release rainbow trout in slow western waters are in trouble with a parasitic disease that causes young fish to spin in circles until they die. Early research indicates a link to the worms in waders priced over $100. Flyfishing elders spinning through assorted mid-wife crises are befuddled on how to match this whirling hatch; a manager of a hatchery contaminated with the infection said, "Hey, at least they're more fun to catch!"

TOURNAMENT FISH

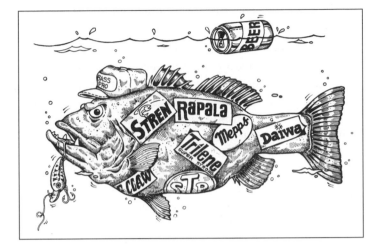

ALIASES: Lunker, hawg

SCIENTIFIC NAME: *Mictropterus salmoides*

PERSONAL STATISTICS: Adults without lead weights average two pounds. With lead weights, they tip the scales at five pounds. Both are around a minimum twelve inches in length.

WHERE TO VIEW: General distribution is wherever bass competitors lie in waiting. Or just lie. The best place is near any gear-banging group activity. The worst place is at the fish fry celebrating the winners at the end of the tournament.

WHEN TO VIEW: At the weigh-in, before the biggest are rolled in beer batter inside the judge's tent.

WHAT TO LOOK FOR: Beer in cans, beer in bottles, beer in barrels.

TIPS TO INCREASE LIKELIHOOD OF SEEING: Follow the beer trucks.

OLD DIET: Worms, insects, frogs.

NEW DIET: Plastic worms, insects, and frogs, crankbaits, spinner-baits.

OLD BEHAVIOR: Getting everything bass-ackwards.

NEW BEHAVIOR: Getting everything back-asswards.

LIKELIHOOD OF SIGHTING IN THE NEW MILLENNIUM: One hundred percent. The business of tournament fishing is booming.

FUTURE: Bass and the other tournament fish are subject to intense fishing pressure once a year, then the big money players move on to yet another fishery. During their brief life in the spotlight, tournament fish live quite well. Once a "keeper" is brought to the boat, it is gently unhooked and placed in an aerated water well which has been treated with a chemical formula that replaces lost slime, treats any kind of bacterial infections, and calms the fighting fish. The tranquilizer reduces the weigh-in jitters of the competitors, finned or otherwise. If a fish dies in transport, competitors place the deceased in their opponent's not-so-live well. Once the fish have been weighed and the snot squeezed out of them, state officials take the smaller ones (ones the judges don't want) for their annual department fish fry, because they know best how to fix them.

HATCHERY FISH

ALIASES: Chump salmon, fish-like fish, farm animals, swimming hot dogs, salt water guppies

SCIENTIFIC NAME: *Oncorhynchus doltus*

PERSONAL STATISTICS: The adults always weigh the same and are about the same length.

WHERE TO VIEW: General distribution is wherever the will to ignore the needs of wild fish is alive and well. The best place is in the Pacific Northwest. The worst place is in the Pacific Northwest.

WHEN TO VIEW: When they surface on a wild stream looking for their hatchery pellets, or when they are being trucked on their migration to the sea.

WHAT TO LOOK FOR: A puzzled look when they see natural foods on the bottom of a wild stream. A good sign of the presence of hatchery fish is the cormorant. These scavengers prefer the easy pickings of concentrated fisheries.

TIPS TO INCREASE LIKELIHOOD OF SEEING: Move to the Pacific Northwest.

OLD DIET: Guppy Chow.

NEW DIET: Second helpings of Guppy Chow.

OLD BEHAVIOR: Bred to be caught by sport and commercial fishermen so they do as they have been programmed. Either that or spawn too early.

NEW BEHAVIOR: Want to return to the hatchery where the fast food is to die for. Instead they bump into the fish ladders that are supposed to lift them past the damn turbines to bathe in the warm backwaters.

LIKELIHOOD OF SIGHTING IN THE NEW MILLENNIUM: One hundred percent. The outrageous lack of cooperation and political will between the interested parties assure a continual supply.

FUTURE: Hatchery biologists continue to experiment with hybrids to meet recreation expectations, while trying to accommodate deterioration in habitat. Hatchery salmon are pre-programmed by hatchery habitat to live in the long concrete aqueducts that drain the Los Angeles basin.

SPECIAL FISH BONUS
How to Help Your Finned Friends
of the Old Millennium

Eat more red meat.

If you must eat whale meat, eat more minke whale meat.

If you don't like minke whale meat, eat more harbor seal meat.

Eat more white meat and the other white meat.

Eat more discounted meat with questionable "sell by" dates.

Eat more from the other food groups, whatever they are.

Recycle. Drink only the broth from shark-fin soup.

Don't eat blue-fin tuna sushi. It's an ignoble end for an American fish whose best friends are diced celery, mayonnaise, a little fresh lemon juice, salt, black pepper, fresh lettuce, and two slices of toasted eight-grain bread.

Don't eat any beluga sturgeon. Beluga whales are another matter, but only after you run out of minke whale.

Don't eat any beluga caviar. Just say no. Unless it's accompanied by a good Russian vodka. And an unemployed Bolshoi ballerina.

INSECTS

There are ten to thirty million invertebrate species, which translates into 99 percent of all animal species. Insects are small, can fly, and are 70 percent of all animal species. The bugs will inherit the earth, especially when all our chemical and genetic experimentation shows up in their genes.

Scientists are experimenting with known behaviors of insects such as tampering with the will of ladybugs to "fly away home." If a ladybug can be reprogrammed through radiation and chemical mutations to just stay home and eat harmful aphids, gardeners and the cloning industry would be much happier. But scientists just don't understand the prairie parable:

Ladybird, ladybird,
Fly away home.
Your house is on fire,
And your children all gone.

It wasn't Lady Bird's fault her daughters weren't pretty and left home. Lyndon wasn't that handsome either. The former president looked like he, not the beagle, had been picked up by the ears.

Geneticists are close to altering insects that carry malaria, dengue, and a host of other insect-borne diseases. The unspoken concern is that such tropical diseases are nature's way of punishing those who were born in a Third World country. Male arachnids are hoping that geneticists will get around to tinkering with black widow behavior.

Even the original play insect has been redrawn for today's child's play. In 1998, the children's game Cootie celebrated a half-century with cosmetic surgery. The simple body, head, two eyes, two antennae, six legs, and a tongue were not snappy enough for the modern buyer so the old cootie, so to speak, now sports high-top sneakers.

In popular entertainment, bugs, and more recently ants, are making anthills out of mountains. Even small independent producers use ant colony behavior to mirror aberrant human behavior, like the adaptation of A. S. Byatt's *Angels and Insects* (1994). The early classics were not so subtle. In the 1950s and 1960s, bugs were the doomsayer's canaries in the mineshaft (probably due to a lack of canaries). The mutations in the movies were typically caused by

contact with radioactive waste or
nuclear explosions, and the fears of
even the scientific community were best
expressed in *Them!* (1954), "Nobody
can predict what we'll find in that
new (post-nuclear) world."

The panic over the Y2K bug is
certainly understandable when you
consider the high-strung
nature of the ordinary pro-
grammer. As anyone who's
stayed in a wilderness cabin
understands, bug bytes are
avoidable by just closing
your Windows.

ANTS (Fire)

ALIAS: Hot damn!

SCIENTIFIC NAMES: *Solenopsis invicta* (red), *Solenopsis richteri* (black)

PERSONAL STATISTICS: Adults are seemingly weightless until
they cover your body. The adult length is a svelte one-eighth to
one-quarter inch long.

WHERE TO VIEW: General distribution is in newly developed areas
in the eleven Southern states. The best place is in an early, less
fiery but nine-foot-long form in the movie *Them!* (1954), with
an early, less intelligent Charlton Heston in *The Naked Jungle*
(1954), and in an early, more intelligent form in *Phase IV* (1973).
The worst place is in your pants, under your tent, near any atomic testing site, in your outside air-conditioner condenser, and in
your free-range ant farm.

WHEN TO VIEW: Any time you go outside in eleven Southern states.

WHAT TO LOOK FOR: Picnickers running in terror from fire-ant
erupting mounds about two feet tall, three feet wide.

WHAT YOU HOPE NOT TO SEE: Multiple queen colonies.

TIPS TO INCREASE LIKELIHOOD OF SEEING: In the affected
eleven Southern states, just go outside.

OLD DIET: Human flesh. When human flesh is unavailable, an occasional bird or Bambi.

NEW DIET: More human flesh, seeds, insects, rodents, snakes, lizards, and anything in and out of its way.

OLD BEHAVIOR: Biting everything in sight in Argentina, Brazil, Paraguay, and Uruguay.

NEW BEHAVIOR: Biting everything in sight in Alabama, Arkansas, Georgia, Florida, Louisiana, Mississippi, North Carolina, Oklahoma, South Carolina, Tennessee, and Texas, and moving in all directions at about five miles a year. One fire ant isn't a problem but a sting quartet is.

LIKELIHOOD OF SEEING IN THE NEW MILLENNIUM: One hundred percent.

FUTURE: The key to the success of fire ants in the new millennium is a rigidly ordered society full of motivated workers (no Dilberts), strike-force soldiers, consort males, and a real Queen. Fire-ant society has a thin red line drawn in dry, southern sand that is defended by ground troops and raids others when necessary.

These South American fire ants originally landed in 1919 in Mobile, Alabama, which made those urban Alabamans much more mobile. The black ants and red ants have produced hybrids that seem able to tolerate the cooler weather northward. Even though fire ants sting mostly those living in warm, humid climates, the pissant Sting can bug music lovers everywhere.

BEE (Killer)

ALIAS: Africanized honeybee (AHB)

SCIENTIFIC NAME: *Apis mellifera scutellata*

PERSONAL STATISTICS: Adults weigh heavily on the minds of the weak. For a long time, too.

WHERE TO VIEW: General distribution is Texas, Arizona, New Mexico, and California, especially Los Angeles. The best place is mid-1970s *Saturday Night Live*, when it was funny, led by John Belushi, and later swarming in *X-Files—The Movie* (1998). The worst place is within a one hundred feet of their hives.

WHEN TO VIEW: There is no good time to view these bees.

WHAT TO LOOK FOR: People running for cover, screaming, swatting at their head and ankles, covering their private parts, and leaving their children or infirmed grandparents as decoys.

TIPS TO INCREASE LIKELIHOOD OF SEEING: Wear bright flowery clothing and shiny jewelry, douse yourself with tropical floral colognes and shampoos, hum Rimsky-Korsakov's *Flight of the Bumblebee*, and swat killer bee nests out of trees.

OLD DIET: South American blood.

NEW DIET: North American blood.

OLD BEHAVIOR: Before mating with European honeybees in Brazil, these African bees were busy as bees, partnering with birds in traditional sex education, which for the birds was for the birds.

NEW BEHAVIOR: Swarming more often, dividing into new colonies, and shaking their bootie in waggle runs about the human harvest to the East and West. Hybrids are ten times more likely to attack than the common honeybee.

Over the centuries, the honeybee hive has stood as a model of the church or state, ideas of order, industry, and charity, and subjects loyal to a queen bee, but even Margaret Thatcher's beehive hairdo failed to impress an unruly electorate. Labor unions promote the rights of the worker bee, yet even the most ardent Hoffa supporters agree that interest in worker issues has been diluted by Dilbert-styled irrelevance.

LIKELIHOOD OF SIGHTING IN THE NEW MILLENNIUM: One hundred percent. In the late 1950s, twenty-six colonies of these killers escaped from a research center near Brazil. By 1990, these illegal aliens had arrived in Texas and have since located in other Southern states.

Like all bees, threatened killer bees release an alarm chemical that tells the other bees to join in the kill. Unless a severe allergy to bee stings is present, one or several bee stings will not kill a healthy human. Thick-skinned Republicans are in the least danger, especially those with the heavy Hyde from that side of the aisle.

About forty persons die from insect bites a year, and half are caused by bees. An old superstition is that if you see a swarm of bees, make a wish and it'll come true. If you see a swarm of killer bees, make that wish on the run.

As soon as you see a swarm rising, run fast and straight. Make a beeline into the largest group of people you can find. Let them share your pain.

FUTURE: The dominant bees of the twentieth century were spelling and quilting bees. The dominant bees of the twenty-first century will be these buzzers.

Scientists predict that domestic honeybees in the southwest will be Africanized early in the new century, giving homegrown conservatives a case of the hives.

Geneticists are trying to isolate the gene that makes the AHB so irritable. Once discovered, the research will be available to nurserymen and marriage counselors. Killer beekeepers will become culinary heroes as they market seasoned killer bee honey with a natural bite.

COCKROACH (German)

ALIASES: Croton bug (German), Ralph, Palmetto bug (American), beetle, water bug

SCIENTIFIC NAME: *Blatella germanica; Periplaneta americana* (American)

PERSONAL STATISTICS: Adults weigh a little bit and average five-eighths of an inch in length.

WHERE TO VIEW: General distribution is everywhere where humans live, especially in urban high-rise buildings, and any New York City street-front restaurant. The best place is in the movies *Joe's Apartment* (1996) and *Bug* (1975), in the short-lived Steven Bochco series *Capitol Critters* (1992), in Don Marquis' Archy and Mehitabel stories, and as a dance in John Waters' *Hairspray* (1988). The worst place is on any serving utensil or in any dish. In *Mimic* (1997), cockroaches were carriers of the contagious Strickler's Disease, which struck children hard. A cockroach-eating Judas breed with an observed reputation for wearing funny shoes was created out of termite and mantis DNA and was doomed like any biological mutant designed to crush the roach. It should be noted that the mantis female devours the head of the male during sexual union, making the male preying mantis pray just a little harder. There is a larger lesson in the movie and if you know what it is, write it on a Post-It note and put it on your refrigerator.

WHEN TO VIEW: They are always there, whenever it's convenient for you. If you see one in the daylight, there are more, lots more. If you feel one in the dark, don't turn the lights on.

WHAT TO LOOK FOR: Walls and ceilings that move when the lights are turned on.

TIPS TO INCREASE LIKELIHOOD OF SEEING: Leave food out.

OLD DIET: Everything, even a cast-off exoskeleton.

NEW DIET: Everything.

OLD BEHAVIOR: Have been know to wash themselves after being handled by people. Smart thinking!

NEW BEHAVIOR: Trying to develop a resistance to boric acid.

LIKELIHOOD OF SIGHTING IN THE NEW MILLENNIUM: One hundred percent, especially in California or any other outpatient smoke-zone. We easily see twenty-five of the four-thousand-plus known species. One healthy cockroach whose young all reproduce will birth 10 million new insects a year.

FUTURE: Cockroaches can exploit a changing urban environment yet have shown little interest in new vacation homes. David Quammen has noted, "the real reason for their long-continued success and excellent prospects is that . . . they never have specialized." They also have the ability to metabolize every variety of poison we spray on them and with the finite number of formulations, we're doomed and they're not.

FLY (black)

ALIAS: Beelzebub (as lord of the flies)

SCIENTIFIC NAME: *Simuliidae*

PERSONAL STATISTICS: Adults never get above flyweight and measure less than 5 mm.

WHERE TO VIEW: General distribution is any vacation on or by the water. The best place is in *The Fly* (1958), that old one with Vincent Price. The worst place is any of the sequels and Cronenberg's goo-fest.

WHEN TO VIEW: Daylight, late spring and early summer.

WHAT TO LOOK FOR: Garbage, stinky garbage.

TIPS TO INCREASE LIKELIHOOD OF SEEING: Go fishing.

OLD DIET: Eye secretions and other body fluids from anyone daring to share their marine environment, especially blue-blooded adventurers.

NEW DIET: All vacationers, especially nouveau riche or retirement-enriched eco-tourists.

OLD BEHAVIOR: Bothering the large ungulates in the wild. Female black flies and no-see-ums cut skin to lap oozing blood for protein to feed their eggs.

NEW BEHAVIOR: Preferring thinner-skinned vacationers' blood to tough moose and elk hide.

LIKELIHOOD OF SIGHTING IN THE NEW MILLENNIUM: One hundred percent.

FUTURE: All the black flies—house flies, deer flies, yellow flies, stable flies—are not easily repelled. "Shoo Fly, don't bother me!" doesn't carry the weight it once did and ordinary salves aren't powerful enough. If you are in a Lund aluminum fishing boat watching a bobber on a calm Minnesota summer day, count on black flies in your ointment.

Black flies are a relative upstart. Fireflies have been around much longer. As Rufus T. Firefly explained in the classic Marx Brothers' *Duck Soup* (1933), "Why, the Mayflower was full of Fireflys. And a few horse flies, too. Fireflys were on the upper deck and the horse flies were on the Fireflys."

The black-faced fly, *Simuliidae aljolson* comes from our theatrical past. Its burlesque behavior guaranteed a short life, yet spawned flights of fancy for many.

MOSQUITO

ALIAS: common domestic mosquito

SCIENTIFIC NAME: *Culex pipiens*

PERSONAL STATISTICS: Empty adults weigh under a pound; once engorged with blood, they bloat up to around a pound. All this and still only a fraction of an inch long.

WHERE TO VIEW: General distribution is every vacation location.

The best place is in the 1993 film classic, *Skeeter,* where illegal dumping of chemicals creates a giant bug, draining the remnants of Michael J. Pollard's film career; and also Paul Theroux's *The Mosquito Coast,* written before V. S. Naipaul bugged Theroux into becoming the Andy Kaufman of expatriate literature. The worst place is inside your mosquito net, and outside your mosquito net along the route to the outhouse.

WHEN TO VIEW: Just before and after sunset. Morning, afternoon, and evening, too. In Alaska, all hours in between.

WHAT TO LOOK FOR: Other vacationers slapping themselves, theme parks closing swimming pools early, staff muttering "encephalitis" under their breath.

TIPS TO INCREASE LIKELIHOOD OF SEEING: Exercise! Sweaty, lactic acid is an major attraction.

OLD DIET: Your blood.

NEW DIET: Your blood.

OLD BEHAVIOR: Spreading malaria, yellow fever, and one hundred other maladies on safaris and other foreign military and religious adventures.

NEW BEHAVIOR: The females still have the blood fever, needing the proteins for her eggs.

LIKELIHOOD OF SIGHTING IN THE NEW MILLENNIUM: One hundred percent.

FUTURE: The mosquito may be our last and best line of defense to the accelerating need to "conquer" wilderness. If so, we should hold a tickertape parade for the new landed immigrant, the Asian Tiger mosquito, *Aedes albopictus.*

SCORPION

ALIASES: Sculptured scorpion, scorpius, fishhook

SCIENTIFIC NAME: *Centruroicles sculpturatus*

PERSONAL STATISTICS: The adults weigh a certain amount and are almost three inches long.

WHERE TO VIEW: General distribution is in warm wet or dry climates, arriving mid-July in the South, low on the horizon. The best place is west of Sagittarius, near Centaurus. The worst place is in your bedroom slippers.

WHEN TO VIEW: Not during the sign of Scorpio when the scorpion's sting is supposed to be more terrible. The ancients believed that the scorpion's sting is particularly menacing to women and worse to virgins. The likelihood of finding a virgin in the New West headquarters of Santa Fe, New Mexico, is, however, small.

WHAT TO LOOK FOR: Your bedroom slippers.

TIPS TO INCREASE LIKELIHOOD OF SEEING: Shake out your bedroom slippers before inserting your feet.

OLD DIET: Insects and spiders.

NEW DIET: Your body mites.

OLD BEHAVIOR: Devious and deadly, the sculptured scorpion is the most poisonous slipper companion in Arizona.

NEW BEHAVIOR: Forceful, mercurial, and often unpredictable, Scorpios are particularly successful and feared in business. Other signs follow Luke 10.19: "Behold, I give unto you power to tread on serpents and scorpions."

LIKELIHOOD OF SIGHTING IN THE NEW MILLENNIUM: One hundred percent.

FUTURE: Old astrologers identified the scorpion as the force behind sexual genitalia and if you were born under the sign that straddles October and November, your organs are out of control. It's not clear how this defense will hold up in today's court but in the new millennium, it'll be easier to beg for forgiveness than ask for permission.

SPIDER

ALIAS: Black widow

SCIENTIFIC NAME: *Latrodectus mactans*

PERSONAL STATISTICS: Adults are light as a feather and measure three-eighths of an inch.

WHERE TO VIEW: General distribution is where you shouldn't be anyway, and in dark, protected places. The best place is near Little Miss Muffet's tuffet, pinned to a 4-H project board, or *The Incredible Shrinking Man* (1957). The worst place is in a beehive hairdo. There once was a blond coed who sprayed her bouffant so hard and high that it would occasionally bump into low hanging branches. This student started to have fainting spells in school and after one spell when she couldn't be revived, was taken to the hospital where a nurse noticed a small spider crawling out of her hair. On the operating table, her hairdo was found to harbor a huge nest of black widow spiders. The moral is blond coeds shouldn't go to school.

WHEN TO VIEW: Just before the fangs penetrate a delicate part of your anatomy.

WHAT TO LOOK FOR: A red hourglass on the back of this tarantula-like insect lowering down inside the mambassa net over your bed. Once the female bites, the hourglass turns upside down and your life will pass before your eyes.

TIPS TO INCREASE LIKELIHOOD OF SEEING: Do your "business" in the outside biffy.

OLD DIET: Insects, especially flies.

NEW DIET: Insects.

OLD BEHAVIOR: Females kill their mates with love and then eat them, putting a whole new spin on that song, "I'm in the mood for love."

NEW BEHAVIOR: Females do not kill mates until child support is clearly in place. Females will not eat their young unless they are really hungry.

BEHAVIOR FAVORED BY MARVEL COMICS: Bitten by an irradiated spider, Spider-Man developed great strength and reflexes, an extra sense for danger, and an ability that allowed him to climb walls. In those crazy days of the early 1960s, when feminism had an extremely sharp sting, it was good at least in a comic sense that only man was bit.

LIKELIHOOD OF SIGHTING IN THE NEW MILLENNIUM: One hundred percent for both the black widow and its poisonous pal, the brown recluse.

FUTURE: The black widow's poison is more potent than the rattlesnake and causes severe skeletal-muscular pain, breathing difficulties, and weakness—symptoms much like those that follow an annual performance review. The female glands increase in size and venom in strength as the black widow ages, which is an awful twist on the social order and not to be emulated.

If E. B. White had set *Charlotte's Web* around the life of a black widow spider rather than the ordinary barn spider, you can bet it would have had a much different ending. Sadder, too.

TICK

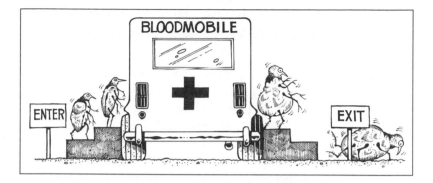

ALIASES: Deer tick, black-legged tick, Western black-legged tick

SCIENTIFIC NAME: *Ixodes dammini* (Northeast and Upper Midwest), *Ixodes scapularis* (Midwest, Southeast), *Ixodes pacificus* (West Coast)

PERSONAL STATISTICS: Adults weigh just a little bit and are smaller than a dime.

WHERE TO VIEW: General distribution is grassy and bushy areas everywhere, waiting for you to brush by the ends of the long grass. The best place is on a whitetail deer. A whitetail deer can carry several hundred ticks *per ear* and half of them can carry Lymes disease. Go ahead, pet that deer in the roadside park! The worst place is on or in your most private parts.

WHEN TO VIEW: As soon as you stop moving outside.

WHAT TO LOOK FOR: Little black bugs setting up blood donation stations in the dark regions of your incontinence.

TIPS TO INCREASE LIKELIHOOD OF SEEING: Go outside.

OLD DIET: Your blood.

NEW DIET: Your blood, up to one hundred times its own body weight.

OLD BEHAVIOR: Crawling into your darkest hiding spots, burying a mouth full of reversed barbs into your fat, soft skin, and bloating on a four-day Slurpee.

NEW BEHAVIOR: Still ticking you off, with the ability to hospitalize you with babesiosis, Colorado tick fever, ehrlichiosis, Rocky Mountain spotted fever, relapsing fever, and tularemia.

LIKELIHOOD OF SIGHTING IN THE MILLENNIUM: One hundred percent.

FUTURE: Tick-borne diseases have a speedy new carrier, the little field mouse, who will go wherever you want to. Once the tick learns there are homes that still have shag carpet to hold onto, the tick will move indoors and the fun begins.

Smaller tick-like insects are also on serious increase. Head lice is very common among schoolchildren and on British movie stars displaying inappropriate behavior along Sunset Boulevard.

MAMMALS

On the ground or in the water, mammals are the most adaptable and diverse group of vertebrates. Whales and dolphins are old salts, while beavers prefer fresh water. On land, there are species that live above ground and others camp out below; bats live above it all. Armadillos, moles, and bats are insectivores, and others crave the action of a carnivorous lifestyle.

Many interesting mammals are not included in this collection. They are typically those least touched by urban sprawl, such as the pronghorn antelope, mule deer, and the Roosevelt elk. Animals in high elevations like bighorn sheep and mountain goats are even out of reach of most vacation homes. There are critters who luckily live in areas where developers can't turn a quick and large profit; others are so cranky, humans are wise to avoid an encounter. The wolverine or "evil one," flees all settlement and makes sure you are all unsettled before departure. Badgers don't like people—even in Wisconsin, the badger state. On the other hand, the large farm animals that winter vacation on the National Elk Refuge in Jackson, Wyoming, want you to like them, even more than you like the Canadian gray wolf. Mammals seem more like us and, as totems, we use their characteristics to inspire our sports teams and sell consumer products. With the menagerie we're moving into the new millennium, this may be inappropriate.

ARMADILLO (Nine-banded)

ALIASES: Texas turkeys, Hoover hogs (during the Depression), official state mascot of Texas

SCIENTIFIC NAME: *Dasypus novemcinctus*

PERSONAL STATISTICS: Adults keep to a trim seven to twelve pounds, and are fifteen to seventeen inches long with a tail about the same size. The Armadillo's penis is about a third as long as the body, which shows you how horny this horny-plated little rascal can get.

WHERE TO VIEW: General distribution is Texas, Oklahoma, Louisiana, Florida panhandle, and most of the Southeast. The best place is as a purse in a gift shop. The worst place is in your azaleas.

WHEN TO VIEW: Most active at night, by the light (by the light, by the light) of the silvery halogen headlight.

WHAT TO LOOK FOR: An anthill that looks more like a molehill.

TIPS TO INCREASE LIKELIHOOD OF SEEING: Disregard drought restrictions and water your lawn. It's your lawn, damn it!

OLD DIET: Earthworms, spiders, termites, scorpions, and antz.

NEW DIET: Any infestation in your new lawn, fire antz.

OLD BEHAVIOR: Blessed with a very small brain, it's smart enough to know not to fight any larger creature that doesn't like its hole-digging; armadillos jump, faint, and curl into a ball or simply tucks its legs under and squats in defense.

NEW BEHAVIOR: The Catholic Church is interested in the armadillo's ability to give birth to quadruplets from one egg.

LIKELIHOOD OF SIGHTING IN NEW MILLENNIUM: In the South, 100 percent. Their low body heat and little insulation prevent a northern expansion.

FUTURE: The little armored thing has a high tolerance for chemicals—an adaptation perfectly suited for a millennium certain to be dominated by drugs.

BAT (brown)

ALIASES: Winged rat, house bat

SCIENTIFIC NAME: *Eptesicus fuscus*

PERSONAL STATISTICS: Adults weigh one-half to three-quarters of an ounce, and are four to five inches in length. Two incisors on the upper jaw, three on the lower.

WHERE TO VIEW: General distribution is throughout most of the United States, except Southern tip of Florida and Southeastern Texas, around your outdoor lights and street lights. The best place is in Grandma's belfry or any other hibernaculum. The worst place is in Grandma's hair as she rakes hay in the field.

WHEN TO VIEW: Early in the morning, out in the field at night, on a full moon, out of hell.

WHAT TO LOOK FOR: Two small incisor marks on Grandma's neck or any other neck, for that matter.

TIPS TO INCREASE LIKELIHOOD OF SEEING: Have Grandma stack her hair while working in the field.

OLD DIET: Insects, Grandma's blood.

NEW DIET: More insects, more of the ol' bat's blood.

OLD BEHAVIOR: Sucking blood out of Grandma's head until she

can't work in the fields and/or fix lunch for the men; the engorged bats then can't fly and must walk on their spindly legs up the stairs to her belfry to let their stomachs settle upside down.

NEW BEHAVIOR: Going batty, running out of grandmothers working out in the field. They just aren't making Grandmas like they used to. Grandma certainly wouldn't approve of baby bats flying with their mouth open.

In Southern climates, some bats don't hibernate at all. Like those who party in the bat caves, they just go into some sort of stupor.

LIKELIHOOD OF SIGHTING IN THE NEW MILLENNIUM: One hundred percent. Over forty species live in North America and even though there isn't as much big-haired field work any more, cities like Austin, Texas, are encouraging the growth of species like the Mexican free-tailed bat for insect control. More importantly, this bat cross-pollinates the agave plant, the essential ingredient in tequila, an important breakfast drink in the Southwest.

FUTURE: Bats eat large quantities of night-flying insects such as mosquitoes, one of the blood-sucking insects of the future. Bats are twice as efficient at locating objects by reflected sound so senior officers in the U.S. Navy are interested in enlisting their sonar abilities to tailhook female candidates. A few of our only flying mammals aren't the brightest lights—witness the fruit bat Stellaluna thinking she was a bird. But bats are smarter than us, sleeping a good two-thirds of their life and able to market their guano. Bats prefer abandoned buildings, which qualifies them as the poster child of inner-city decay.

BEAR (black)

ALIASES: Smokey, Teddy, Winnie, Yogi (Jellystone)

SCIENTIFIC NAME: *Ursus americanus*

PERSONAL STATISTICS: Adults weigh two hundred to seven hundred pounds and are 4½ to 6½ feet in length. Bears seem longer when the length stands up and woofs.

WHERE TO VIEW: General distribution is Alaska, south through the Rockies, east to northern tier states, small populations throughout south, and a very "smokey" subspecies in Yellowstone National Park. The best place is in a box of animal crackers. The bear is the only species with two postures in the Barnum collection—one standing and one sitting—but the way the crackers dump load the boxes, you may only get one. The worst place is inside their den, where a sow with cubs would put a good scout spin on the term den mother.

WHEN TO VIEW: At their convenience. A black bear's view is limited by poor eyesight. Can you imagine the frustration of being the big dummy that "went over the mountain, to see what he could see" and the "other side of the mountain was all that he could see"? This frustration leads to inappropriate behavior best controlled by a fifty-five gallon tank of red pepper spray.

WHAT TO LOOK FOR: A U.S. Forest Service parade float.

TIPS TO INCREASE LIKELIHOOD OF SEEING: Rub peanut butter on window sill; fry a pan full of bacon with the window open and exhaust fan turned on high up at the lake cabin; wear bells on clothing as park bears respond to dinner bells that, as your life flashes before you, toll for thee.

TIPS TO DECREASE LIKELIHOOD OF SEEING: Run a pack of Karelian bear dogs outside your cabin. Stay home, locked up in your room.

OLD DIET: The original three preferred porridge. Yogi, a cartoon mutant, preferred picnic basket food. Visiting bears from darkest Peru enjoy marmalade. Black bears from the land of sky-blue waters enjoy a tall cold Hamm's.

NEW DIET: Corn, melons, berries, *Ulee's Gold* (1998), prickly pear cactus fruit, feed pellets for horses or horses full of pellets. Hal Jam, the literary bear in *The Bear Went Over the Mountain* ordered pies, ice cream, pitchers of honey and maple syrup, cakes, and Cheesy Things on the cuff of a New York publishing house. Less literary bears like oats for breakfast.

OLD BEHAVIOR: Endlessly answering the question about its call of nature in the woods. In the fall, bears eat large quantities of food, then plummet into an extended state of inactivity. This coincides with the football season in which the oxygen intake of other sloth-like creatures is halved and heartbeats slow until touchdowns.

NEW BEHAVIOR: Smokey is over fifty years old and like other boomers, suffers from typical aging problems: memory loss, and inappropriate behavior in impromptu social settings. Stand your ground should you take an informal meeting. The black bear likes to bluff and old Smokey may forget why he's charging you. If you draw a young boar, you won't forget his charging you. If you draw Sonny "the Bear" Liston, you lose.

To decrease your likelihood of being eaten, let your spouse stand his or her ground, or let your "cubs" go play with theirs. If a black bear decides you are the plate du jour, one bite of your nasty hide will return the carnivore to a diet of moth larvae and pine tree nuts.

To increase your likelihood of eating black bear, go to Taiwan and put your mitts on some bear paw soup. The brew is alleged to create sexual vigor. The market for other spare parts in Asian folk medicine is equally strong. Wildlife enforcement agents estimate that for each bear killed legally in the United States, another is poached. However, for many palates poached bear is much too tough. A cub is preferred.

LIKELIHOOD OF SIGHTING IN THE NEW MILLENNIUM: One hundred percent. For the price of a Twinkie, it's easy to find a big park bear hug.

The likelihood of sighting a humanized brown-phase black bear in the new millennium depends on if the Ewoks return in any of the *Star Wars* prequels.

The likelihood of being bitten by a black bear in the new millennium is less than being bitten by a wild horse, yet pound for pound, horse meat is much too tasty to waste as bear bait.

FUTURE: The teddy bear, a black bear named after the first President Roosevelt (and not a popular feminine undergarment), can and will be found wherever stuffed animals are held in captivity. Teddy Ruxpin is a lost voice in that retail wilderness. Black bears living in Yellowstone during the big fire of 1988 are still really black.

BEAR (brown)

ALIASES: Grizzly, Alaskan brown, Kodiak bear (on Kodiak Island), Bart, the white bear, Great bear, silvertip (old male), Bruno, Lucky

SCIENTIFIC NAME: *Ursus arctos horribulus*; *Ursus arctos middendorffi* (Southern Alaska)

PERSONAL STATISTICS: HUGE. Adults smash the scales at three hundred to twelve hundred pounds, averaging four hundred to five hundred for males, and three hundred pounds for females. They range from four to nine feet in height and you don't want to see them standing tall, especially the nine-footers of Alaska, the last frontier. If you encounter one of the heftier females with cubs, you will become a grizzly statistic.

WHERE TO VIEW: General distribution is Alaska and northern Rocky Mountains, especially Montana and Yellowstone National Park. The best place is in the movies *Legends of the Fall* (1994), *The Edge* (1997), and *The Great Outdoors* (1988); behind bars in a zoo; at a great distance; on the California State Flag; behind a fat photographer at McNeil River State Game Sanctuary; Katmai National Park; and the Karluk Lake Brown Bear Sanctuary. The worst place is against all odds, climbing up your tree; if you are a rancher in the Bitterroot or North Cascades ecosystems; in the Big Blue House; in the Hundred Acre Wood; and, as Frank Craighead advises in *The Track of the Grizzly*, under three hundred feet away in open country. (Cinematic Note: Bart, a trained grizzly, was the star of both *The Edge* and *The Bear* (1992). Does anyone who doesn't secretly wear Victorian undergarments really think Anthony Hopkins is a match for even a trained bear?)

WHEN TO VIEW: When they are not viewing you. Avoid all eye contact. It's considered impolite in bear society to stare at one another. A well-mannered grizzly will not tolerate bad manners.

WHAT TO LOOK FOR: Fresh bear sign (scat or poop), torn-up dirt or logs, stripped bark or claw marks on standing trees, magpies in a tree, a partially eaten jogger. If you have fresh human poop in your pants, a grizzly mom and her cubs just crossed your path.

TIPS TO INCREASE LIKELIHOOD OF SEEING: Pick up a seemingly abandoned cub for a real Kodiak photo opportunity. Hang your camp meat one foot off the ground. Sleep in the same clothes you wear while frying your bacon. Practice snorkeling upstream during the salmon spawning run. Reel in a big river fish in bear country. Leave your blueberry preserves open on the picnic table and/or crash through the berry bushes making woofing sounds. Throw used tampons or sanitary pads in the bushes.

TIPS TO DECREASE LIKELIHOOD OF SEEING: Sing Slim Whitman's songs as loud as you can. It'll hurt the bear's ears, too.

OLD DIET: The word grizzly comes not so much from the white hair tips that gives the bear a grizzled appearance as the scraps of human gristle left from intense human/brown bear interaction.

Other foods: picnic baskets and other park garbage, a freshly dumped city or national park dump, fish entrails, and food of the last resort: white bark pine seeds, wild berries, and moth larvae.

NEW DIET: Before the griz go into hibernation, they are hungry as a bear and eat all day long, consuming up to ninety pounds (twenty thousand calories) a day. A bear only has a half-year to fatten up for the Big Sleep, so the desire for food is commanding. In areas where humans intrude on bear habitat, there are now noticeable quantities of red pepper spray on their natural forage, which has created an animal taste for more spicy foods.

OLD BEHAVIOR: Playing with butterflies and eating.

NEW BEHAVIOR: There are reports of young grizzlies in Yellowstone deciding not to hibernate, giving the snowshoe and cross-country ski community the squirts.

Should a young male grizzly block your path, disregard the warning never to stare at a bear. Your survival odds increase should the male bear misinterpret your stare as a "copulatory gaze" and assume you are a hairless Canadian hybrid brought in by wildlife managers.

LIKELIHOOD OF SIGHTING IN THE NEW MILLENNIUM: Seventy-five percent. Grizzlies will eat their young to survive (which gives them the most human of characteristics). Should the grizzly become more like the black bear, by losing its traditional disinterest in humans, we may see more than we want of this humanivore.

The likelihood of a grizzly sow putting her cubs in daycare in the new millennium is around 0 percent, give or take a few.

FUTURE: The griz got his early scientific name (*horribilis*) the hard way—he earned it. General H. Norman Schwarzkopf got his sobriquet "the Bear" the same way. From an all-too-brief employment as role model for Disney's Bear Country USA and roughhouse playmate of Mr. Adams, the grizzly smarts horribly from the Yellowstone Park decision to close the garbage dumps and does not want to return to the old diet of grubs and roots when there are ample hunters, joggers, and other succulent back country users to gnaw on.

The real danger will come from the escape of offspring of

grizzlies being displayed in the privately operated bear parks, especially those located in Southern climates. These studio bears live in air-conditioned pens as small as two hundred square feet and are "rotated" throughout the day, from pen to exercise area to facing the public. Once on the loose, these park bear "experts" will gladly take their rightful place behind bars.

In an age of uncertainty, only grizzly bears are absolutely guaranteed to succeed in the new millennium.

BEAVER

ALIASES: Bucky, eager

SCIENTIFIC NAME: *Castor canadensis*

PERSONAL STATISTICS: Adults waddle at thirty-five to seventy pounds and lie flat at twenty-five to thirty inches, with a flat tail up to ten inches long

WHERE TO VIEW: General distribution is at the best damn sites all over the United States, except the arid Southwest. The best place is on Sharon Stone in *Basic Instinct* (1992), and in a very good hat store. The worst place is living on an adjoining wildlife preserve while doing its damn best to flood your tree farm.

WHEN TO VIEW: At night.

WHAT TO LOOK FOR: Unexpected flooding, trees chewed a foot off the ground, and a cone-shaped stick and mud house in the middle of your swimming pool.

TIPS TO INCREASE LIKELIHOOD OF SEEING: A well-placed leghold trap will give you a leg up on the little landscape architect.

OLD DIET: Certain trees and woody plants such as aspen and pine, and a wide variety of herbaceous and aquatic plants.

NEW DIET: Certain designer trees and woody plants ordered by less talented two-legged community planners.

OLD BEHAVIOR: This native American was minding its own business and doing what it damn well pleased until the seventeenth and eighteenth centuries when it became prized for its svelte felt atop the heads of the fashionable and military. Abe Lincoln saved their skin by wearing a silk hat to his inauguration. Recent revelations about Thomas Jefferson indicate an earlier presidential interest in a similar fur-bearer.

NEW BEHAVIOR: Still busy as a beaver, blocking any running water (even the water you pass), and building the best water barriers by a damn site. If you want a cost-effective, permit-free obstruction, *Leave It to Beaver!*

LIKELIHOOD OF SIGHTING IN THE NEW MILLENNIUM: One hundred percent.

FUTURE: Much like developers, beavers modify their environment to fit their needs. Yet beavers have no profit motive and, at no cost to the owner, provide fresh, new habitat to fish and other wildlife. America's First Stewards of the Land, whose consulting fees are damn site larger, use every lethal means to snuff out Mother Nature's very best environmental engineers. Though you'd have to be a real butt-head to bet against a marine mammal that lives upstream.

BISON

ALIASES: Buffalo, monarch of the plains, plains buffalo, Hornaday's bull, black diamond, *Le Boeuf* (French), breakfast/lunch/dinner (Native American)

SCIENTIFIC NAME: *Bison bison*

PERSONAL STATISTICS: Adults weigh between sixteen hundred and twenty-two hundred pounds, but for a more concrete example, a sixty-ton proud yet inanimate buffalo grazes at Jamestown, South Dakota. Adults are usually ten to twelve feet in length, and up to six feet tall at the shoulder.

WHERE TO VIEW: General distribution is in various national wildlife refuges, parks, and on private property. Yellowstone National Park has the nation's largest unfenced herd. The best place is in the movie, *Dances With Wolves* (1990), the National Bison Range in Montana, and, if they ever fix the roads, in Yellowstone National Park. A sure place is at the border where park buffalo migrate north out of the park for greener pastures. The worst place to view is filling the panoramic viewfinder of your disposable camera.

WHEN TO VIEW: While they are lying down or if standing, when their tails are down, swinging to and fro. Do not view when the bulls are "in the rut" and their tails and other appendages are erect.

WHAT TO LOOK FOR: Parked Winnebagos and their windbag occupants.

TIPS TO INCREASE THE LIKELIHOOD OF SEEING: Buy a Yellowstone Day Pass and follow the ambulances to the Winnebago parking lots. To increase the likelihood of seeing the white buffalo, the active use of any native hallucinogen should work.

OLD DIET: When Bill Cody was still active, it was dirt sandwiches, prairie grasses, and lame Indians on foot.

NEW DIET: Managed habitat grasses, lame tourists under foot.

OLD BEHAVIOR: In the old West, buffalo were the passive, unwilling participants in the largest animal slaughter by "the man." The bison came to America over a million years ago via a land bridge across the Bering Sea and if the water weren't so deep during Bill Cody's Wild West, they would have returned.

NEW BEHAVIOR: Commercial interests are crossing the buffalo with domestic cattle, creating a more manageable yet tasty "cattalo" or "beefalo." The early word on this three-eighths bison domestication is unclear. One half the herd in Yellowstone is suspected to carry brucellosis, a disease the cattlemen of the North do not want passed to their charges, so park residents avoid "snapshots" in southwest Montana. Snowmobile emissions originating in West Yellowstone, Montana, pre-smoke the herd before it moves north on groomed track.

LIKELIHOOD OF SIGHTING IN THE NEW MILLENNIUM: Excellent, with more than 150,000 now in private and public herds nationwide. We need the buffalo in the new millennium because we need one true nomad in our animal arsenal.

FUTURE: The largest American "unmanaged" herd in Yellowstone National Park has caused more human injuries than all other species, including Yogi and Smokey the Bear. This rate of injury is expected to increase once this herd catches the ill northeast wind of Jane Fonda and Ted Turner's efforts to create a larger national appetite for buffalo burgers.

The safest place, now and then, to view a buffalo is on the flip side of an old Indian-head nickel. If you try to have your picture taken sitting on a buffalo, your life isn't worth a plugged one.

CAT

ALIASES: Feral cat, *chat sauvage* (French), *Wildkatze* (German), Fritz the Cat (underground), the other white meat (feral dog)

SCIENTIFIC NAME: *Felis catus*

PERSONAL STATISTICS: Adults six to fifteen pounds in weight and twenty-four to thirty-six inches in length.

WHERE TO VIEW: General distribution is anywhere feral dogs aren't. The best place is grinning on the tree branch in *Through The Looking Glass*. The worst place is in Cleveland Amory's posthumous memoir, *The Bludgeoned Cat: My Last Will and Testament.*

WHEN TO VIEW: In the evening.

WHAT TO LOOK FOR: Dead songbirds, batty old cat lovers in sneakers, large hairball with songbird parts.

TIPS TO INCREASE LIKELIHOOD OF SEEING: Stake a songbird out in the yard or place cat food or milk along the edges of the greenbelts and woods lining city parks.

OLD DIET: Songbirds. That something-the-cat-dragged-in was your favorite songbird. In his first appearance, Fritz the Cat was a rock star who ate a teenage-girl pigeon, which to New Yorkers on a park bench is a songbird.

NEW DIET: White mouse ragout with wild mushrooms, prepared by Feral Friends of the Cat. Once the feral cat is full, it continues to kill more songbirds just for sport.

OLD BEHAVIOR: Eating as many songbirds as possible before impartial researchers are able to take an accurate count. If your cat looks like it swallowed the canary, it probably did. Unfortunately, a long cinematic tradition of alley cats such as O'Malley in *The Aristocats* (1970) has created a sympathetic audience for males catting about the neighborhood, looking for open nursery windows to suck the breath from sleeping infants. Except within a safe circle around the barnyard, feral cats fear rural living; with coyotes moving into the city, they fear for the worst. Nine lives will not be enough.

NEW BEHAVIOR: No predictable cat-and-mouse games; wild, yet still co-dependent with sympathetic cat-lovers. The life span of a feral cat is not more than two years, so their love-making abilities accelerate, with females reaching sexual maturity at five months, short gestation periods of two months, and several litters a year. The humans who feed feral cats in the park never reach maturity, much less sexual maturity.

In the real world, the Northwestern Wildcats wouldn't only beat, they'd EAT the Golden Gophers of Minnesota.

LIKELIHOOD OF SIGHTING IN THE NEW MILLENNIUM: One hundred percent.

FUTURE: There are an estimated sixty million pet cats in the United States and half of them spend some time outside killing songbirds. There are an estimated thirty to fifty million feral cats that spend *all* their time outside killing songbirds. Cat lovers don't believe this. They think all cats are more like Lillian Jackson Braun's sleuth Koko. Songbird lovers think that feral and songbird-eating domestic cats should be more like Laverne's Boo-Boo Kitty—stuffed. It's unknown if feral cats can land on their feet when thrown or accidentally fall from on high. The only way to test this theory is from atop a grain silo or old growth timber.

COYOTE

ALIASES: Trickster, prairie or brush wolf, barking dog, Wile E.

SCIENTIFIC NAME: *Canis latrans*

PERSONAL STATISTICS: Adults weigh twenty to fifty pounds, slightly more in the East where they mate with wolves and other immigrants. They measure thirty-two to fifty inches in length with a ten- to fifteen-inch tail.

WHERE TO VIEW: General distribution is in all lower forty-eight states, particularly in South Dakota, the Coyote State, and in almost every habitat, but not in Hawaii, except when various subspecies from the species PAC, C.O.Y.O.T.E. are cited in the lobbies of big convention hotels. The best place is in any suburban shadow around any Western city. The worst place is at your picnic table, in your dog kennel.

WHEN TO VIEW: In the dawn's early light, some enchanted evening, near any spring pasture full of livestock.

WHAT TO LOOK FOR: Tracks around your Weber grill.

TIPS TO INCREASE LIKELIHOOD OF SEEING: Don't clean the grill, leave old charcoal hardened by drippings in bowl, let your pets out at night, leave your trash out on the curb the night before pick-up, use wide mesh on the bottom of your rabbit hutches, stake lambs at night in an open field.

OLD DIET: Juniper berries, acorns, apples, peaches, corn, and all melons, rabbits, watermelons, beetles, grubs, snakes, lizards, rodents above and below ground, insects, ducks, domestic turkeys, Bambis, more Bambis, and especially newborn antelope.

NEW DIET: Any lamb that looks like a newborn antelope, any cat or dog that looks like a newborn antelope, any pet in Westchester County that looks like a newborn antelope.

OLD BEHAVIOR: Foiled by roadrunners and fooled by other hapless animals on Saturday morning cartoon hell. Coyotes like to steal other predator foodstuffs, but as the backwoods bruin in William Kotzwinkle's *The Bear Went Over the Mountain* claims, "you have to bang them against a tree real hard, which knocks the wind out of them. Then they behave."

NEW BEHAVIOR: Chasing hapless suburban animals all the live-long day, doo-dah, doo-dah. Interested in reclaiming small rural towns caught in the agribusiness pincher. No longer fooled or foiled. Will not deign mating with lesser suburban canines. Prefers to mate with wolves but the latest Canadian arrivals in Yellowstone are unfamiliar with American dating behavior. The new coyotes are applying for associate membership in the National Sheep Herders Association, posing as cattle herd dogs. The bravest urban coyotes are the healthiest, and their progeny are urban renaissance dogs that love to harmonize with fire and ambulance sirens.

LIKELIHOOD OF SIGHTING IN THE NEW MILLENNIUM: In a western suburb, 99 percent in the first month; other locations, 99 percent in the first year. (In either location, add 1 percent for presence of a Weber grill.)

FUTURE: City departments of animal regulation take thousands of complaint calls a year about "inappropriate" coyote behavior. Expect the hours of the Coyote Café to expand. Their adaptable behavior, panache, chutzpah, and social system guarantee survival.

Population control only stimulates increased reproduction and immigration. Everything the federal government threw at the coyote couldn't eradicate the high plains drifter. This urban guerrilla and equal opportunity eater has evolved into a super-sly dog with a cultivated taste for flame-broiled steaks—fearless and capable of great patience, one coyote will decoy the rube in the barbeque apron while another turns the steak on the grill—hard to trap, and harder to poison, even with a large overdose of Worcestershire Sauce.

DEER (whitetail)

ALIASES: Virginia Deer, Bambi, camp meat

SCIENTIFIC NAME: *Odocoileus virginianus*

PERSONAL STATISTICS: Adults range from one hundred to three hundred pounds in weight and six to seven feet in length.

WHERE TO VIEW: General distribution is wherever home gardeners take pride. The best place is in your neighbor's decorative shrubs and flowering plants. The worst place is in yours, in your headlights.

WHEN TO VIEW: Dawn, dusk.

WHAT TO LOOK FOR: Shredded, jagged greens, cracked acorns.

TIPS TO INCREASE LIKELIHOOD OF SEEING: Place a salt block in your neighbor's decorative shrubs. To decrease likelihood of seeing, scatter mountain lion poop on your bushes.

OLD DIET: Acorns, fresh fruit, wild berries, fruit trees, vegetables—in particular, sweet corn, especially with sweet butter—wildflowers, leaves, twigs, and buds of woody browse plants such as oak.

NEW DIET: Bushes where songbirds used to sit and sing lovely tunes, ground cover that used to provide cover for ruffed grouse and bobwhite quail, your prize roses and azaleas.

OLD BEHAVIOR: Except for the odd Disney attempt to portray a whitetail's woodsy life as something comic, the whitetail deer is a typical herd animal.

NEW BEHAVIOR: Delighted with the long decline of wolves and the mountain lion. Concerned about their reintroductions and relaxation of bans on hunting, either with or without dogs.

LIKELIHOOD OF SIGHTING IN THE NEW MILLENNIUM: One hundred percent. There are over twenty million whitetail in forty-three states, so any motorist is likely to run into one. Deer whistles on your fenders will alert them to your arrival.

The likelihood of Disney's Bambi wanting to live in Felix Salten's *Bambi: A Life in the Woods* is around 0 percent.

FUTURE: The explosive population growth of whitetail deer and their tick-carrying subspecies in its fractured former habitat combined with the new landlord's Bambi-mentality has created an omnipresent "hoof-rat" with a taste for neighborhood shrubbery, ornamental plants, and fruit trees. Overcrowding in the suburban deer delis cause heavy-hoofed competition for the tastiest greens and decorative flowers, yet neighborhood covenants continue to require tasteful replacements. The mentality of development landscape review boards guarantees a rosy future for these flower eaters.

DOG (feral)

ALIASES: Bad doggie (suburbs), wild dog from hell (rural)

SCIENTIFIC NAME: *Canus unfamiliaris biteyourassofficus*

PERSONAL STATISTICS: Adults weigh up to 150 pounds and over, and are three to four feet in length. Smaller dogs are too smart to test the wild; the guard morons such as pit bulls, German shepherds, and Rottweilers also avoid the unpredictable wild.

WHERE TO VIEW: General distribution is outside the soft-focus homes of those who open a can of chicken soup for their pet-like souls. The best place is with mad Englishmen out in the hot sun, on Indian reservations, in the crosshairs of a scoped rifle. The worst place is killing "Maa" in the original *Babe* (1995) and certainly not in *Lady and the Tramp* (1955).

WHEN TO VIEW: Before, during, and after the dog days of summer. Feral dog life is short, measured in reverse domestic dog years. A one-year-old feral dog should have been dead seven years already.

WHAT TO LOOK FOR: Your pampered pet's empty collar.

TIPS TO INCREASE LIKELIHOOD OF SEEING: *Go outside!*

TIPS TO DECREASE LIKELIHOOD OF SEEING: None. Forget about it. They're here.

TIPS TO DECREASE LIKELIHOOD OF BEING KILLED: *Do not* attempt to break up a fight between a wild dog and your domestic pet. Just go inside and reserve a plot at the local pet cemetery. You'll need a bit of the hair of the dog, any dog, after such an event.

OLD DIET: Any rural mammal.

NEW DIET: Any rural, suburban, and urban mammal. Feral dogs don't suffer the swings in availability of wild game. They know what time small pets are put out to go poo, and failing that, know which day the garbage is picked up.

OLD BEHAVIOR: Mean as "junkyard dogs," guarding the dump. Old Yeller was not a feral dog, he was a high-concept pet. Stray dogs on the big screen don't stray far from the studio catering truck.

NEW BEHAVIOR: Being much more a pack animal, harassing urban deer, going postal on uniformed employees. The best place for a feral dog is as trim on a winter parka.

LIKELIHOOD OF SIGHTING IN THE NEW MILLENNIUM: One hundred percent.

FUTURE: Recent DNA analysis suggests that wolves came indoors for food and shelter as long as 135,000 years ago. Since that day, dog brains have shrunk substantially in proportion to their size, particularly in the smaller breeds. The surviving behavior is yapping, incessant yapping.

Researchers believe that wolves warmed to humans as more dominant wolves. The domesticated wolves saw that begging for food or cooperative feeding of young had a high value. Wild dogs demonstrate few preferred human characteristics. There are no warm, wild-dog human-interest stories on the six o'clock news, and artists don't wax eloquently about a wild dog field-stripping a ewe. Are wild dogs just symptoms of our rootless society? Perhaps, but any dog that learns to accept drinking out of a toilet fits the Republican end-user profile for the Clean Water Act.

The dog we don't want to see go feral in the new millennium is the miniature dachshund. Once a feral wiener cleans out the rabbit, mole, and groundhog holes, he'll be coming after you.

DOLPHIN (bottlenose)

ALIASES: Flipper, "big chicken of the sea" (San Diego tuna fleet)

SCIENTIFIC NAME: *Tursiops truncatus*

PERSONAL STATISTICS: Adults weigh over three hundred pounds, and are up to ten feet in length.

WHERE TO VIEW: General distribution is the Atlantic coast. The best place is in the movie *Flipper* (1963), two sequels, and a TV series; on the sides of pinball machines; on the fifty-yard line of Joe Robbie's stadium in Miami, Florida; basking in the Las Vegas sun in as close a simulation of their natural habitat as possible in the middle of the desert at the Mirage Hotel; and atop the Twin Dolphin Hotel at Disneyworld. The worst place is on active duty in the U.S. Navy underwater demolition units, or in *The Day of the Dolphin* (1973).

WHEN TO VIEW: The movie and TV sequels can usually be found on cable between 3 and 4 A.M.

WHAT TO LOOK FOR: Hiding behind schools of tuna.

TIPS TO INCREASE LIKELIHOOD OF SEEING: Sing, "They call him Flipper, Flipper, faster than lightning . . . ."

OLD DIET: Mullet, eels, and squid.

NEW DIET: When their agents can find them big screen work, stunt doubles enjoy the change from a wild diet to the fresh sushi prepared by the studio catering truck.

OLD BEHAVIOR: As the sailor's friend, guiding lost boats to safe harbor. The bottlenose dolphin prefers the friendly coast and the sensibilities of those who own beachfront homes.

NEW BEHAVIOR: High-concept script has boy finds and loves dolphins, adults want to hunt dolphin, boy saves dolphin and hopes for less fishy movie roles. Dolphin, too.

LIKELIHOOD OF SIGHTING IN THE NEW MILLENNIUM: One hundred percent.

FUTURE: Ever threatened by drift-net tuna fishermen in the South Seas, the bottlenose dolphin prefers staff positions in resort hotel dolphin encounters. In Hawaii, Florida, Mexico, and Bahamas pools, well-heeled patrons can "come close, look into their eyes" and "feel the strong attraction" through hands-on flipper contact with worker mammals lacking a resort retirement package. Recently, the highly imitative dolphins have tried to return the affection, much to the embarrassment and messy inconvenience of all the well-heeled, two-legged mammals in the pool.

FOX (21st Century)

ALIASES: Red, Mr. Fox

SCIENTIFIC NAME: *Vulpes vulpes*

PERSONAL STATISTICS: Adults weigh seven to twenty pounds and average about ten pounds. The fox is thirty to forty-five inches long, including tails that run two-thirds the length of the body.

WHERE TO VIEW: General distribution is most of United States, except for much of the Southwest, Southern Florida, and the Rockies. The desert subspecies was lost during World War II. The best place is in front of your hounds. The worst place is in your chicken coop.

WHEN TO VIEW: Dark, dusk.

WHAT TO LOOK FOR: Chicken feathers.

TIPS TO INCREASE LIKELIHOOD OF SEEING: Bring out the hounds.

OLD DIET: Flies, angleworms, grasshoppers, rabbits, hares, birds, small burrowing animals, and summer vegetation.

NEW DIET: Chicken, whole or in parts, original recipe preferred.

OLD BEHAVIOR: An import from England, this small canine needed few survival skills to stay ahead of a bloated rural gentry on horses.

NEW BEHAVIOR: Outfoxed by coyotes in the wild, the red fox concentrates on picking the locks at the industrial chicken farms.

LIKELIHOOD OF SIGHTING IN THE NEW MILLENNIUM: One hundred percent.

FUTURE: Playing a tiny but fabled part in the decline of the small chicken farm, the red fox is the most abundant and widely spread fox in North America. When pressured, the red fox spreads out widely in the fractured environment, with a behavior that triggers anglophilic equestrians, "the unspeakable," to gallop in full pursuit after "the uneatable," with dogs and horns that have no place in a modern orchestra. The only real safety for a red fox is the local ASPCA chapter or, most recently, the British Labor party.

The twenty-first century fox will never measure up to the Foxx that ruled the genus *Comic genius* during much of the twentieth century. Redd was an alpha male who could be found wherever comedy pushed and prevailed. One  of the best places to see him is in *Cotton Comes to Harlem* (1970), the role that led to his starring in *Sanford and Son*, the American version of the popular British comedy *Steptoe and Son*. The likelihood of seeing the older and best Redd Foxx in the new millennium is only in reruns. In 1991, Redd finally joined Elizabeth.

GROUNDHOG

ALIASES: Woodchuck, marmot, whistle pig, Punxsutawney Phil, Buckeye Chuck (Ohio), French Creek Freddy (West Virginia), General Beauregard Lee (Georgia), Wiarton Willie (R.I.P.). The folk etymology of the word *groundhog* is an actual woodchuck sound; Chamber of Commerce executives made it into a compound word that best describes the Babbits hogging the ground above this shy, horny mammal.

SCIENTIFIC NAME: *Marmota monax*

PERSONAL STATISTICS: Adults are four to fourteen pounds in weight and sixteen to thirty inches in length.

WHERE TO VIEW: General distribution is Midwest and Eastern United States. The best place is in the movie *Groundhog Day* (1993). The worst place is in your garden.

WHEN TO VIEW: Midway between winter solstice and spring equinox, February 2 or Candlemas day every year, generally early morning. Or late afternoon if you are in Pennsylvania or a like state of mind. If filming one of those dull Groundhog Day events, don't forget to have the local fire department run the four-inch hose down the groundhog's rear exit off camera.

WHAT TO LOOK FOR: Bill Murray.

TIPS TO INCREASE LIKELIHOOD OF SEEING: Go to a video store and look under Bill Murray.

OLD DIET: Greens, roots, tubers, seeds.

NEW DIET: The food scraps around the network catering trucks.

OLD BEHAVIOR: If the meteorological marmot sees his shadow on a bright, sunshiny day, he will hole up for six more weeks of winter. If not, spring will come early or the animal has too much fresh dirt in its eyes.

NEW BEHAVIOR: With tunnel vision typical to underground dwellers, the woodchuck has difficulty seeing his shadow in the glare of all the media klieg lights, especially when all he wants to do is chuck his woodie with a member of his opposite sex.

LIKELIHOOD OF SIGHTING IN THE NEW MILLENNIUM: Fifty percent.

FUTURE: Researchers have discovered that woodchucks are good models to study liver cancer and hepatitis, a sure indication "Chucky" is a regular guy, a model citizen for the new century. With a less than 40 percent accuracy rate on weather predictions, this forecaster matches the ability of all others on the small screen, guaranteeing employment well into the twenty-first century.

HORSE (feral)

ALIASES: *Chevale tartare* (Paris restaurant), wild horse, mustang (when they were hot, like in the sixties), adult hobbyhorses posing as Phantom, Pied Piper, Misty

SCIENTIFIC NAME: *Equus caballus*

PERSONAL STATISTICS: Adult males weigh 800 to 850 pounds; the females slim down to 600 to 750 pounds. Each will yield two five-pound rump roasts. Adults are usually five feet high, with the Eastern horses smaller.

WHERE TO VIEW: General distribution is Southwest United States, particularly Nevada on the Bureau of Land Management's herd-management areas. Two herds of wild ponies that, according to one legend, are descendants of carnival carousel ponies live at the Assateague Island National Seashore and in Chincoteague National Wildlife Refuge off the coast of Maryland and Virginia. The best place is in the West at a BLM auction, at the annual Wild Pony Swim and Drowning off Chincoteague Island, at a Denver home football game, with *pommes frites*, and in a one-horse town in the horse latitudes. The worst place is running fast and free across pre-softened, overpriced sports apparel.

WHEN TO VIEW: Running off into the sunset, bridle gear bouncing behind.

WHAT TO LOOK FOR: Export trucks full of shaggy, small beasts that up close and without soft focus do not look at all like the Black Stallion.

TIPS TO INCREASE LIKELIHOOD OF SEEING: Go to Reno, Nevada, which, unfortunately, has one of the handiest populations.

OLD DIET: Taxpayer grasses reserved largely for low-cost cattle leases.

NEW DIET: Taxpayer grasses reserved largely for low-cost cattle leases and sea oats that hold fragile dunes in place.

OLD BEHAVIOR: Even in the horse-and-buggy days, the wild horse had no social skills. Not even a good whisperer could lead a feral horse to water. Even they seemed to know it was the iron horse that helped defeat Crazy Horse. This behavior led cowboys to bourbon and water.

NEW BEHAVIOR: Using much more horse sense, opting for the feral to domestic transfer through the federally sponsored adopt-a-horse program. Wild horses were domesticated by the Mongols who sought wider territory, and now their descendants are going wild, ridden by the mongoloids that prefer polo.

LIKELIHOOD OF SIGHTING IN THE NEW MILLENNIUM: Fifty percent.

FUTURE: Since 1973, the Bureau of Land Management has operated an adoption service for some fifty-five thousand wild "orphan" mustangs. (Wild horses didn't know they were orphans until *Misty* [1961]-eyed Americans saw the movie.) Qualified moms and dads are allowed four "orphans" a year at $125 each, with clear title at the end of the first year if they are good surrogate parents. Whoa be to those who adopt a dominant stallion. Unlike his distant, domesticated cousin, the wild horse remains resolutely wild and new parents sedate the newest family members with attention deficit disorder drugs.

Attention Robert Redford fans: Any whispering to a feral horse will be neigh-sayed! But then again, Redford's sun dance around nature is a horse of another color.

MOLE

ALIASES: Eastern, Mister, common

SCIENTIFIC NAME: *Scalopus aquaticus*

PERSONAL STATISTICS: Adults weigh three to six ounces and are three to eight inches in length with an inch-long tail.

WHERE TO VIEW: General distribution is most everywhere, other than the hard-packed Rocky Mountains and Great Basin. Best place is in Kenneth Grahame's *The Wind in the Willows*, in the Cotswalds, and next to Roald Dahl's house. The worst place is in your yard.

WHEN TO VIEW: When they come up for air after you've connected the fire hose up to their back door.

WHAT TO LOOK FOR: Holes connected to tunnels just below the ground.

TIPS TO INCREASE LIKELIHOOD OF SEEING: Plant new grass or lay new sod, hook up ground vibrators to a city power line.

TIPS TO DECREASE LIKELIHOOD OF SEEING: Pave your yard, let the Jack Russell terrier out.

OLD DIET: Insects, vegetables, worms, grubs, slugs.

NEW DIET: More of the above.

OLD BEHAVIOR: Making mountains out of molehills.

NEW BEHAVIOR: Making molehills out of mountains.

LIKELIHOOD OF SIGHTING IN THE NEW MILLENNIUM: One hundred percent.

FUTURE: Not to be confused with the restaurant menu term "molé" or Cindy Crawford's face wart. In the absence of Cold War grand espionage, moles are more likely to be found in dusty John Le Carré novels than in East Berlin. In a suburban future of carefully manicured lawns, the mole has expanded habitat. Able to dig tunnels at fifteen feet per hour, the mole can easily change direction should trouble be close. The mole's future would be rosier if tunneling was concentrated in less conspicuous backyards.

MOOSE

ALIASES: Bullwinkle J., elk (Europe)

SCIENTIFIC NAME: *Alces alces*

PERSONAL STATISTICS: Adult males weigh nine hundred to fourteen hundred pounds, the females seven hundred to eleven hundred pounds. Both are about 7 to 10 feet long, and 6 to 7½ feet high.

WHERE TO VIEW: General distribution is in the meadows, streams, and willow thickets of Maine, Minnesota, Northern Michigan, Alaska, the Rocky Mountains. The best place is at Jackie Gleason's lodge, on a popular Canadian lager. (For those looking for

Bullwinkle J. Moose, call Frostbite Falls, Koochiching County, Minnesota.) The worst place is on a dark, rainy night, going 100 mph around a bend in the road, when your headlights flash on a large, dark object lifting out of a low wetland.

WHEN TO VIEW: Dawn, dusk.

WHAT TO LOOK FOR: Big, dark, goofy-looking animals.

TIPS TO INCREASE LIKELIHOOD OF SEEING: It'll be a surprise.

OLD DIET: Willow (birch and aspen) leaves and twigs, aquatic plants during summer, bark and branches of beech trees, and a sweet tooth for sugar maple during the winter.

NEW DIET: More willows, especially willows seasoned by road salt.

OLD BEHAVIOR: Retiring, solitary, often cranky, chewing on a cud all day, with nary a deep moose thought.

NEW BEHAVIOR: Still very obstinate, won't even back down from that bull horn announcing the light at the end of the train tunnel, more proof of low membership in the moose Mensa Society.

LIKELIHOOD OF SEEING IN THE NEW MILLENNIUM: One hundred percent.

FUTURE: The moose is generally unaffected by human encroachment because developers, America's First Stewards of the Land, don't like to build homes on stilts. Moose food sources are, however, threatened by exploding populations of elk, and their children are concerned with the reintroduction of wolves.

MOUNTAIN LION

ALIASES: Cougar (Pacific Northwest), panther (Eastern United States), puma (South America), catamount (New England), Klandagi—"Lord of the Forest" (Cherokee), Ghost Walker, painter (Southern variant of panther)

SCIENTIFIC NAMES: *Felis concolor* (cat of a single color)

PERSONAL STATISTICS: Adults weigh anywhere from 80 to 250 pounds, averaging 140 to 150 pounds, and are about forty to sixty inches long with a thirty- to thirty-six-inch tail, standing tall at twenty-six to thirty-two inches at shoulder.

WHERE TO VIEW: General distribution is throughout North America. The best place is at your Ford/Mercury dealer where a sporty new Cougar is waiting for a test drive, along the western range of the Sierra Nevada Mountains, suburban developments, and green belts and park trails in twelve western states (no telling which twelve). The worst place is in Southern Florida, where a small subspecies is limping along with fewer than fifty members suffering from the genetic injustices of inbreeding, and any place you wear your new deerskin jacket.

WHEN TO VIEW: Dawn, dusk.

WHAT TO LOOK FOR: Scratch marks on tree trunks and the wall carpets in your family room that are at least four feet above the ground or floor.

TIPS TO INCREASE LIKELIHOOD OF SEEING: Start feeding deer, move your game farm, sheep, and/or cattle into their old neighborhood, let your young wear a Tiger costume while trick-or-treating in the suburbs, drink out of the river on all fours.

OLD DIET: Deer, especially nuisance urban and suburban deer that have been relocated back into the "wild" or any other animal five times its weight.

NEW DIET: Any calf that acts/looks like a deer, any human that acts/looks like a deer, any pet that acts/looks like a deer, any jogger that acts/looks like a deer, and finally any Californian that acts/looks like a deer.

OLD BEHAVIOR: Shy, reclusive, wary of dogs and people.

NEW BEHAVIOR: Sly, inclusive, prefers dogs and people.

LIKELIHOOD OF SIGHTING IN THE NEW MILLENNIUM: One hundred percent. The prospects are high that *you* will be that special something the cat dragged in.

FUTURE: The quiet population explosion of the catamount is tantamount to a short-fuse time bomb. Not anxious to give up its mountain vacation home, especially where the tasty desert bighorn lives, inexperienced sub-adult lions venture out into settled areas, shopping for the freshest meats at the suburban deli counter. Just wait until these young puddytats grow up and teach their cubs the ropes. There'll be no need to reintroduce these feral cats.

MOUSE (wild)

ALIAS: deer mouse

SCIENTIFIC NAME: *Peromyscus maniculatus*

PERSONAL STATISTICS: Adults weigh three-eighths of an ounce to one and one-half ounces and are five to eight inches in length.

WHERE TO FIND: General distribution is widespread, with the notable exception of the Southeast. The mouse in Orlando is a non-native hybrid. The best place is in the children's book, *Poppy* by Avi. The worst place is in your dusty cabin in the Four Corners region of the United States, in Lyme, Connecticut.

WHEN TO FIND: Whenever is good for you is good for them.

WHAT TO LOOK FOR: Droppings.

TIPS TO INCREASE LIKELIHOOD OF SEEING: Go outside.

OLD DIET: Depending on subspecies and habitat, Rice Chex, Wheat Chex, fruit cocktail.

NEW DIET: Depending on subspecies and habitat, seeds, nuts, small fruits, corn, insects.

OLD BEHAVIOR: Living a coyote-fox-wolf-eat-mouse world. But this is no different inside. A cat can kill up to twenty-four mice a day, which is bad news for foxes and owls who eat what they catch.

NEW BEHAVIOR: Our perception of the mouse is led by the mouse-keepers down at the Magic Kingdom. Even Mickey is being "modified" for the new millennium. Stay tuned.

LIKELIHOOD OF SIGHTING IN THE NEW MILLENNIUM: One hundred percent. The likelihood of dying from diseases carried by deer ticks that live on deer mice is less than 1 percent. Once infected, the likelihood of dying from the hantavirus carried by deer mice in the Southwest is 50 percent. The likelihood of dying from embarrassment for thinking the animals in Disneyland are real is 100 percent.

FUTURE: The house mouse (*Mus musticus*) has supreme domestic survival skills as shown in *Mouse Hunt* (1997), yet wait until the wild mouse comes indoors! The mouse has the unfortunate habit of contaminating that which it can't use—no wonder the mouse easily morphed into a cultural icon.

NUTRIA

ALIASES: Coypu, *ragondin* (French)

SCIENTIFIC NAME: *Myocaster coypus*

PERSONAL STATISTICS: Adults weigh up to twenty-five pounds and are up to four feet long, including a foot-long tail.

WHERE TO VIEW: General distribution is in the Southeast (largest population), now found in Washington, Oregon, and other isolated areas. The best place is in Louisiana, in muskrat houses, and beaver lodges. The worst place is in Louisiana as a "reintroduced" foodstuff.

WHEN TO VIEW: As they scatter when the levee breaks.

WHAT TO LOOK FOR: Less-aggressive muskrats moving out.

TIPS TO INCREASE LIKELIHOOD OF SEEING: Get out the john boat.

OLD DIET: Up to twenty square miles of coastal wetland in Louisiana alone, each year, burrowing into banks and eating the roots and then tops of grasses and aquatic plants.

NEW DIET: Following a rice entrée, this eating machine has a sweet tooth for sugar cane.

OLD BEHAVIOR: Avoiding the fur trade. When the principal source was South America, coats were made from the belly fur, a pelt with a thick, rich underwool from an animal that lives in rivers, half-covered by the cooler water.

NEW BEHAVIOR: Not pleased with Louisiana's Department of Wildlife and Fisheries promoting nutria as food. Paul Prudhomme didn't need to compare the taste and texture of nutria to turtle meat either. Others say rabbit. In an early awareness program, Chef Paul whipped up a nutria etouffé. Since the original Louisiana population were escapees from the McIlhenny farm, use Tabasco as a seasoning.

LIKELIHOOD OF SIGHTING IN THE NEW MILLENNIUM: One hundred percent if you look at the fur jackets being sold in Eastern Europe.

FUTURE: Nutria will be the direct beneficiary if we'll need another Louisiana to house our growing population. Like rabbits, the nutria will eat its own poop to ingest remaining nutrition while resting—a model behavior for the crowded new millennium.

OPOSSUM

ALIASES: Virginia possum, Brer Possum, Pogo Possum

SCIENTIFIC NAME: *Didelphis virginiana*

PERSONAL STATISTICS: Adults weigh up to five pounds and are thirty to forty inches in length, including a foot-long tail.

WHERE TO VIEW: General distribution is originally Southeast, now most anywhere in United States, Pogo in Okefenokee Swamp. The best place is along the roadside. The worst place is along the roadside.

WHEN TO VIEW: Early evening.

WHAT TO LISTEN FOR: Gary Synder reciting, "The Dead by the Side of the Road."

WHAT TO LOOK FOR: Squish marks along side of road.

TIPS TO INCREASE LIKELIHOOD OF SEEING: Go for a drive early evening.

OLD DIET: A veritable eating machine, ignoring nothing.

NEW DIET: Anything a raccoon eats.

OLD BEHAVIOR: Playing possum, hanging around upside down.

NEW BEHAVIOR: No longer content with just playing possum. A very senior opossum is only seven years old; the life processes of a marsupial with an appetite that knows no boundaries will accelerate.

LIKELIHOOD OF SIGHTING IN THE NEW MILLENNIUM: One hundred percent. Of all the lower order of mammals, the seemingly less intelligent animals, opossums will thrive, which gives you some idea of which human behavior will be most valuable in the twenty-first century.

FUTURE: Until opossums understand why the chicken or, for that matter, anyone crosses the road, opossums are destined to be born dead by its side.

If lost in the woods, follow an opossum. They will find the road!

OTTER

ALIAS: Sea otter

SCIENTIFIC NAME: *Enhydra lutra*

PERSONAL STATISTICS: Adults weigh forty-five to seventy pounds, and are thirty to sixty-five inches long, averaging four feet.

WHERE TO FIND: General distribution is in Southern Alaska and the Aleutian Islands (northern population), and along the central coast of California (southern population). The best place is in the water, banging two rocks together. The worst place is in the water, eating abalone that belongs on your table.

WHEN TO VIEW: Abalone is good to eat all day.

WHAT TO LOOK FOR: Out-of-work abalone fishermen.

TIPS TO INCREASE LIKELIHOOD OF SEEING: Paddle in a sea-kayak.

OLD DIET: Clams, abalone, crabs, abalone, fish, abalone, sea urchins, abalone, mussels, and abalone.

NEW DIET: They eat a quarter of their weight daily; their increasing size from eating so many abalone requires even more abalone meat.

OLD BEHAVIOR: Diving, swimming, eating, grooming, and playing with themselves.

NEW BEHAVIOR: Playing with the Furry-Handed Friends of the Otter until even they believe their own cuteness.

LIKELIHOOD OF SIGHTING IN THE NEW MILLENNIUM: Ninety-nine percent on the southern population. The California numbers are slipping and their designation may be switched from threatened to endangered. Once official notification has been received by the abalone fishermen, the "slipped" population will stop hiding in the kelp beds. Or behind emptied crab pots.

Ninety-nine percent on the northern population. Orca whales near the Aleutians have found that sea otters are a small but tasty substitute for the seals and sea lions missing from their traditional food sources swept clean by factory fishing.

FUTURE: Cloth coats just aren't warm enough when that winter wind comes whipping off Lake Michigan. Furbearers ought to know that.

PIG (wild)

ALIASES: Feral hog or swine, Pig pig, razorback, Piney-Woods rooter, Russian boar, Roto-Rooter

SCIENTIFIC NAME: *Sus scruffy scrofa*

PERSONAL STATISTICS: Adults weigh three hundred to five hundred pounds, and measure 3½ to 5 feet.

WHERE TO VIEW: General distribution is in at least eighteen states, primarily South/Southeast from Texas to Florida; in many habitats—woodlands, grasslands, wherever water and cover are. The best place is on a football field at the Arkansas state university. The worst place is in your backyard "natural habitat." The most impossible place is at Disney's Animal Kingdom, since a wild pig was the reason Old Yeller had to be put down. That doesn't mean the Animal Kingdom isn't a wild experience and the McRib Sandwich isn't "a wild taste that allows McDonald's customers to experience the fun and magic of the Animal Kingdom without going to Orlando."

WHEN TO VIEW: On a full-moon night.

WHAT TO LOOK FOR: Rootings, scat, wallows, tree rubs, beds. If you see a rub line that's over six feet tall, leave the area at your earliest convenience.

TIPS TO INCREASE LIKELIHOOD OF SEEING: Don't carry a weapon in wild pig country.

OLD DIET: Whatever they can root: nuts or "mast," bulbs, forbs, berries, bark, marsh vegetation, snakes, and other dead stuff, carrion, too.

NEW DIET: New corn, corn mash "flared" with brew and berries.

OLD BEHAVIOR: A mix of domestic pigs and introduced Russian boars from Europe, the wild pig has a wide range of physical and behavioral characteristics. The most dominant trait is a pigheaded need to root and wallow.

NEW BEHAVIOR: With no real enemies once they reach three hundred pounds, the wild pig is free to roam wherever they please, even to the top of Pork Chop Hill.

LIKELIHOOD OF SIGHTING IN THE NEW MILLENNIUM: One hundred percent in the South and Southeast.

FUTURE: Never try to teach any pig, much less a wild pig, to sing. It wastes your time and annoys the pig. It's also quite likely the pig will excel and you'll be out of the job. What drives most pigs wild is being forced to race in circles at state fairs. Pigs resent being thought of as dogs and other lesser animals.

Scientists look to transplant domestic pig organs with new genetic roots into humans, bypassing the possibilities of rejection. It sounds like a good idea, but there is a chance the procedure would introduce viruses unique to pigs to the human subjects. If the medical community wasn't so pigheaded about using farm rather than wild donor stock, we could end up with people not to be truffled with.

PORCUPINE

ALIASES: Porky, Porky Pine (Pogo), quill pig, *porc espin* (French)

SCIENTIFIC NAME: *Erithizon dorsatum*

PERSONAL STATISTICS: Adults weigh in from seven to forty pounds and stretch from twenty-four to thirty-six inches long.

WHERE TO VIEW: General distribution is most of Western United States, very top of the Great Lake states, and New England. The best place is up in the trees. The worst place is under the family dog.

WHEN TO VIEW: At night.

WHAT TO LOOK FOR: The family dog with quills in his nose and mouth.

TIPS TO INCREASE LIKELIHOOD OF SEEING: Put a salt lick in a neighbor's bushes.

OLD DIET: Any woody materials including ax handles, toilet seat covers, and leather goods such as old shoes with a human salty sweat; in summer, ice fishing houses; in the winter, wooden deer stands.

NEW DIET: Since the increased use of manufactured materials, such as plastic toilet seats and worse, indoor plumbing and metal ax handles, porkies have had to rely more on green plants in the summer and the inner bark of trees in the winter.

OLD BEHAVIOR: Retiring, avoiding the attention of the fisher, another member of the weasel family, that can successfully porque out.

NEW BEHAVIOR: Living behind a reputation of throwing their thirty-thousand-plus quills, this solitary rodent conquers its shyness in its taste for salt. As Ereth in Avi's *Poppy* confessed, "Salt, I can't get enough of it. I'm mad for it. I'd die for it."

LIKELIHOOD OF SIGHTING IN THE NEW MILLENNIUM: One hundred percent.

FUTURE: The second largest rodent in North America will continue to get into prickly situations.

RABBIT (Lucky)

ALIASES: Peter, Bugs, Brer, Roger, Crusader, Ricochet, Benjamin Bunny, Thumper, Velveteen, Coney (fur trade), Flopsy, Mopsy, and Cottontail (Beatrix Potter), Bunny (Captain Kangaroo), White Rabbit (Lewis Carroll), Hazel, Fiver, and company in *Watership Down*

SCIENTIFIC NAME: *Sylvilagus floridanus*

PERSONAL STATISTICS: Adults weigh two to four pounds; without lucky feet, subtract two to three ounces per foot. Rabbits grow to fourteen to seventeen inches long; without lucky feet, subtract three to four inches.

WHERE TO VIEW: General distribution is brushy areas, grown-over fields across Eastern United States (except New England), west through North Dakota, south to Texas, hard left to Louisiana, north by northwest through the briar patch. The best place is Matt Groening's *Life in Hell*, hopping through the briars of John Updike, out of a magician's hat, and best place of all in a flaky crust with potatoes, peas, and carrots, covered in a rich gravy. The worst place is in your herb garden.

WHEN TO VIEW: Twilight, dawn/dusk, but best on Valentine's Day.

WHAT TO LOOK FOR: Carrot tops. Carrot Top, however, is over the top in sight gags.

TIPS TO INCREASE LIKELIHOOD OF SEEING: If a young buck subscribes to the rakish rabbit's *Playboy*, the answer to "What's up, Doc?" will be obvious.

OLD DIET: Anything Old McGregor and McDonald plants in his garden and farm: carrots, peas, lettuce, strawberries, beans. Mr. McGregor's diet included Peter's father who was planted "in a pie by Mrs. McGregor."

NEW DIET: Since the "pie affair," all flour-making products, herbaceous plants in summer, woody varieties in winter.

OLD BEHAVIOR: Playing tricks on Brer Bear, making him as mad as a March hare, breeding like there was no tomorrow (there will be no tomorrow if and when Elmer Fudd's aim improves). Originally the hare's foot had magic power, but due to a confused European public, the rabbit's abundance gave them a foot up on the competition.

NEW BEHAVIOR: When the rabbit puts its best foot forward, it works like a charm.

LIKELIHOOD OF SIGHTING IN THE NEW MILLENNIUM: One hundred percent. The rabbit's proclivity particularly in urban captivity guarantees their future. Bobcat Goldthwait's take on Mr. Floppy deserves a future.

FUTURE: Pete Cottontail is delighted with the revival of hobby farming and small-plot, inner-city horticulture. His elders are not delighted with the new rabbit dishes on trendy restaurant menus and easily see through the use of foreign terms such as *hasenpfeffer*. The family is even more concerned that the new abundance of spare parts will energize a dormant good-luck charm market.

RACCOON

ALIAS: Masked bandit

SCIENTIFIC NAME: *Procyon lotor*

PERSONAL STATISTICS: Adults weigh fifteen to thirty pounds; golf-course members weigh up to fifty pounds. Both are three to four feet long with tail.

WHERE TO VIEW: General distribution is swampy marshland most anywhere in the United States, except the Western mountains. The best place is any golf course community. The worst place is on the deck doing the Heimlich maneuver on your pet for a tasty morsel.

WHEN TO VIEW: At night, particularly on a full moon; in a coon's age.

WHAT TO LOOK FOR: Food wrappers.

TIPS TO INCREASE LIKELIHOOD OF SEEING: Move the cat and dog dish off the deck, just inside the sliding glass door.

OLD DIET: Baby raccoons require a high-protein diet and prefer sweet corn, melons, fruits, silage piles, harvested fields, shellfish, fish, birds, bird eggs, snakes, crops, grapes (both red and green), worms, grubs.

NEW DIET: Adult raccoons prefer whatever retired golfers eat; the second choice is whatever retired golfer's pets eat, which often is better than the former, and lawn fish meal. A good meal for an adult raccoon is two Quarter Pounders or whatever is on special that day.

OLD BEHAVIOR: Raccoons have long been attracted to shiny metal, a trait that trappers quickly seized upon. During the 1920s, raccoons wrapped gay behavior in stadium and motoring coats. In the late 1960s Lyndon Johnson asked the military to bring home a "coonskin for the wall," yet he couldn't save his own political skin soon after.

NEW BEHAVIOR: Likes to climb decks, vines on house. Raccoons seem to understand that their life span in captivity or simulated near a golf course is twice what a coon's age might be in the wild. The raccoon's insinuation into the suburban community is so complete that they don't feel the need to go through the motions of washing their food or hands, much less brushing their teeth, after eating. If they washed up before every meal, they'd start stealing hand lotion. Regarding personal cleanliness, it should also be noted that unlike Mr. Badger's, Mr. Raccoon's den is not kept very clean.

LIKELIHOOD OF SIGHTING IN THE NEW MILLENNIUM: One hundred percent.

FUTURE: This masked marauder is a welcome first-time guest to the patios of golf-course retirees, where a bowl of cat chow is quick work for this four-legged garbage disposal unit. Raccoons are quick learners and, where pet food is not easily found, have petitioned trash can manufacturers for easier-to-operate foot controls and less heft in garbage bags.

RAT (brown)

ALIASES: Norwegian, Ratso, Water rat, Ben, Asiatic rat, sewer rat

SCIENTIFIC NAME: *Rattus Norvegicus*

PERSONAL STATISTICS: Adults weigh ten to twenty-four ounces and are five to ten inches long, plus a seven- to eight-inch tail.

WHERE TO VIEW: General distribution is across entire continental United States, with specific concentration in the rat's nest politicians call their workplace. The best place is in the movie *Willard* (1971) and the sequel *Ben* (1972), with Michael Jackson singing the title song. The worst place is as King of *Where the Wild Things Are* in a ball-buster of a holiday performance near the Norwegian section of Seattle.

WHEN TO VIEW: Anytime during the Chinese Year of the Rat (every twelve years, starting in 2008).

WHAT TO LOOK FOR: Droppings, smudge marks of dirt and oil from their skin, gnawed wood.

TIPS TO INCREASE LIKELIHOOD OF SEEING: Carry your own dishes back to the kitchen in a big-city restaurant.

OLD DIET: Omnivorous, eating any and everything, and then contaminating with its turds any and everything it cannot eat.

NEW DIET: Human food with a fondness for take-out, but even Norway rats don't eat lutefisk. They will eat cat and dog feces. Go figure.

OLD BEHAVIOR: Jumping from sinking ships, acting as rat-finks, ratting out their friends, running in a pack but since the bell tolled for old Blue-Eyes, it's "ring-a-ding-dong, baby!"

NEW BEHAVIOR: In the city, the rat race has metamorphosed into urban marathons, where the freshly carbo-loaded Spandex-clad blindly follow the Pied Piper du jour of exercise. In the suburbs, wrestling squirrels for the best bird seed.

LIKELIHOOD OF SIGHTING IN THE NEW MILLENNIUM: One hundred percent plus. There is at least one rat for every person now and the albino variant of the brown rat is a favorite lab animal and pet. The rat of the new millennium is Raskolnikov, as portrayed in Jerome Charyn's *Citizen Sidel*, who "squeals like a soprano singing inside a tunnel made of tin" at the sight of Marianna, a twelve-year-old girl who bakes butterscotch cookies for the vice president-to-be.

FUTURE: In the unruly world governed by politicians and lawyers, and the spin doctors assigned to their health, the behavior of the rat is no longer extraordinary. The Year of the Rat is a hundred-year calendar.

SASQUATCH

ALIASES: Sasquatch (Salish), Hairy Ghost, Bigfoot, Oma (Hopi), Big Ole (Norwegian)

SCIENTIFIC NAME: *Giagantapithicus blackie* or *Homo troglodyte* or *Delirium tremors imago*

PERSONAL STATISTICS: Adults weigh seven hundred to one thousand pounds and stand seven to eight feet tall with observer blood alcohol of .08 or less, ten to fourteen feet tall with observer blood alcohol way above .08.

WHERE TO VIEW: General distribution is in areas of high per capita alcohol consumption. The best place is near Willow Creek, California, and any other Northern California wooded area with hallucinogenic mushrooms, most any area in the Pacific Northwest without a Starbucks, at any monster car race and/or crushing. The worst place is on a grainy security video from your back yard, in Roger Patterson's 1967 Bluff Creek video, in a Pizza Hut commercial.

WHEN TO VIEW: In the gray twilight when shadows rule and cocktail parties on the deck begin.

WHAT TO LOOK FOR: A big foot; if attached to a big body, run. A large, hairy, smelly bipedal humanoid (other than the immediate family); in the 1967 Roger Patterson film, "a strongly human face" was evident to some, if you think an oblong ape face looks human. A large pile of number two, which could belong to Bigfoot or more likely the observer.

TIPS TO INCREASE LIKELIHOOD OF SEEING: Grain alcohol. More grain alcohol.

OLD DIET: Unknown. Early indications were, if pressed, they wanted to eat your lunch.

NEW DIET: Unknown. Since they live in evergreen forests where edible vegetation is sparse, the diet is most likely baby spotted owls and marbled murrelets.

OLD BEHAVIOR: Shy, reclusive, retiring, picking up after one another as they migrate north/south. Walking very lightly on hard ground until they get near Willow Creek, California, where they leave footprints in modeling clay. Uses park toilet facilities at night, taking great care to lift lid when going number one.

NEW BEHAVIOR: Bigfoot is unlikely to appear without a Diane Fosse first willing to live in close intimacy.

LIKELIHOOD OF SIGHTING IN THE NEW MILLENNIUM: With revived popularity of martinis, Sasquatch sightings will become more common in the metropolitan areas. Sightings/tracks have been made in all fifty states; for the ordinary and more important sober, gainfully employed American, a Bigfoot is as likely (and useful) to be sighted as J. D. Salinger, whose literary footprint is equally suspect. More sightings are expected in Canada but all reports from our Northern neighbor are tied to their currency and discounted up to 40 percent. Until the Himalayan

Forest Service approves the new chair lifts, it's unlikely to see Bigfoot's alpine cousin, the Yeti.

FUTURE: Leif Erickson described sighting hairy, ugly monsters on his first landing on North America. Unfortunately, identical words were used to describe his Swedish crew members. Cryptozoologists are more kind and hopeful as they feed an inexhaustible American appetite (especially for parents trying to keep the kids in the tent) for a friendly large animal. The urban homeless play a similar role.

The majority of sightings that took place in Northern California occurred at peak recreational pharmaceutical usage and the combustible mix of drugs and alcohol that drives American culture guarantees a future populated by Sasquatch.

SEAL (harbor)

ALIASES: Common, hair, earless, leopard seal, Hershel (Seattle)

SCIENTIFIC NAME: *Phoca vitulina*

PERSONAL STATISTICS: Adults weigh 175 to 300 pounds and are four to six feet long.

WHERE TO FIND: General distribution is coastal water, both coasts. The best place is Marinelands of all sorts. The worst place is in the fish ladders of endangered species, in an offshore fish farm.

WHEN TO VIEW: During endangered fish species migrations.

WHAT TO LOOK FOR: Untidy, gutted, threatened, and endangered fish carcasses.

TIPS TO INCREASE LIKELIHOOD OF SEEING: Visit the Seattle locks.

OLD DIET: Fish, mollusks, squid, crustaceans.

NEW DIET: Threatened and endangered fish species, up to ten pounds per day per seal.

OLD BEHAVIOR: Gregarious, feeding on trapped fish on incoming tides.

NEW BEHAVIOR: Quietly, quickly, returning to the feeding frenzy—no matter how often and expensive a forced removal—in California native waters.

LIKELIHOOD OF SIGHTING IN THE NEW MILLENNIUM: One hundred percent.

FUTURE: The harbor seal is in safe harbor indeed.

SHARK (Great White)

ALIASES: Man-eater, Killer shark, White shark

SCIENTIFIC NAME: *Carcharodon carcharias*

PERSONAL STATISTICS: Adults weigh up to twenty-five hundred pounds, and can be up to forty feet long and growing.

WHERE TO VIEW: General distribution is Atlantic and Pacific coasts. The best place is in *Jaws* (1975), *Jaws 2* (1978), *Jaws 3-D* (1983), the Red Triangle off the coast of California. The worst place is *Jaws 4: The Revenge* (1987).

WHEN TO VIEW: Whenever the great land shark of *Saturday Night Live* resurfaces.

WHAT TO LOOK FOR: Big chunks of Robert Shaw.

TIPS TO INCREASE LIKELIHOOD OF SEEING: Tow your cat behind the boat as bait, act like a seal when you swim in the surf.

OLD DIET: Seals, porpoises, whale pups, large fish, wood surfboards and their human attachments.

NEW DIET: Seals, porpoises, whale pups, large fish, plastic surfboards and their human attachments.

OLD BEHAVIOR: The largest marine people eater and proud of it; clean-up on the original Titanic crew and passengers.

NEW BEHAVIOR: Still the largest marine people eater and proud of it; prefers boat and plane accidents of Titanic proportions in warm water.

LIKELIHOOD OF SIGHTING IN THE NEW MILLENNIUM: One hundred percent.

FUTURE: White sharks have been content to be an unpredictable open sea predator, showing up only for casting calls off the beaches of tony East Coast resorts. Once they learn how big the catch is upstream in urban drainage ditches, the alligators are going to have to move over.

Vitamin A from shark-liver oil has been found to be effective in shrinking human hemorrhoids. If the vitamin is still in the shark's liver when you encounter a great white, your hemorrhoids will do more than shrink.

SHEEP

ALIASES: Sheep dip, double dip, double date (high mountain country), Basquette

SCIENTIFIC NAME: *Ovis ditto aries*

PERSONAL STATISTICS: Whether or not they've donated their oysters, adult males will weigh up to 250 pounds; ewes stay closer to 150 pounds.

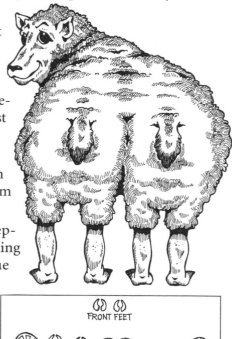

WHERE TO VIEW: The best place is as a Brooks Brothers' double-breasted lamb's wool sweater, as a double-cut lamb chop, in double-thick wool carpet. The worst place is fleecing the public elsewhere.

WHEN TO VIEW: Crossing in front of your Dodge Ram truck.

WHAT TO LOOK FOR: Shepherds (woolly bullies) tending their flocks, large Basque populations.

TIPS TO INCREASE LIKELIHOOD OF SEEING: Having double vision.

OLD DIET: Grass.

NEW DIET: Double helpings of most anything.

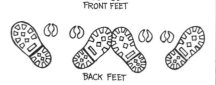

OLD BEHAVIOR: Shorn of any dignity, sheep were once crossed with goats. These unfortunate progeny were called "geeps" rather than

the preferred "shoats," a term protected by the Porcine Actors Guild.

NEW BEHAVIOR: Cloned sheep behavior is unpredictable but assume that you can at least double the old behavior if not in intensity, in occurrence.

LIKELIHOOD OF SIGHTING IN THE NEW MILLENNIUM: One hundred percent. The likelihood of sighting Dolly's namesake in the new millennium is another 100 percent. Should cloners be able to use a few of Dolly Parton's mammary cells, count on your TNN stock splitting.

LIKELIHOOD OF VIRGIN WOOL IN THE NEW MILLENNIUM: Zero percent.

FUTURE: A typical wildlife watcher is more likely to see the domesticated animal than the mountain big horn. These flatlanders are easier to view and, with one black for every one hundred white animals, certainly easier to count—at least before shearing. The media attention given to Dolly and her clone-heads guarantees an additional fifteen minutes of fame but the original *Babe* movie pulled the wool from our eyes. The sheared brain power of this herd animal remains constant from one generation to the next and demonstrates why wild sheep avoid species reunions. No need to ruminate on this future.

SKUNK

ALIASES: Common, black martin, Pepe Le Pew, Flower

SCIENTIFIC NAME: *Mephitis mephitis*

PERSONAL STATISTICS: Adults weigh 1½ to 5½ pounds and are eleven to fifteen inches, plus an elegant ten- to fifteen-inch tail.

WHERE TO VIEW: General distribution is all over the continental United States. The best place is under your neighbor's house. The worst place is under your house.

WHEN TO VIEW: In winter, often seen foraging during the day, usually at night.

WHAT TO LOOK FOR: Noxious inflammable gas clouds.

TIPS TO INCREASE LIKELIHOOD OF SEEING: Light a match.

OLD DIET: Omnivorous, 70 percent animal: insects such as

grasshoppers and crickets in summer, small animals, and reptiles; 30 percent vegetable: berries, buds, grasses, but not skunk cabbage.

NEW DIET: Human food such as melons, sweet corn, whatever the more aggressive raccoon leaves behind.

OLD BEHAVIOR: In a U-shaped defensive position, a skunk can shoot its n-butyl mercaptan cologne up to fifteen feet with fearful accuracy.

NEW BEHAVIOR: Knowing its only serious predator, the great horned owl, is immune to skunk musk, the skunk is petitioning for an open owl-hunting season. Skunks are great kidders and often good pets; *but whatever you do, do not pull their finger!*

LIKELIHOOD OF SIGHTING IN THE NEW MILLENNIUM: One hundred percent.

FUTURE: The white skunk stripe has become a high-fashion hair accent among modern men. Noxious gas will continue to be a part of male social activities, especially in campus frat houses and hunting camps. Fishing camps, too. But not flyfishing camps. Flyfishermen are too camp to fart.

The stripe skunk does not use its breath-stealing secretions against its rivals, only its enemies. The shrinking habitat guarantees a change of behavior.

SQUIRREL (gray)

ALIAS: Tree rodent

SCIENTIFIC NAME: *Sciurus carolinensis* in the East; *Sciurus griseus* in the West

PERSONAL STATISTICS: Adults weigh 1½ to 1¾ pounds and are sixteen to twenty-two inches long.

WHERE TO VIEW: General distribution is urban or heavily wooded areas from roughly Minnesota to the south and east; for the western, along a narrow band from California to Washington, hardwood forests especially oak and hickory. The best place is city parks. The worst place is building a nest from frayed electrical wires in your attic.

WHEN TO VIEW: As soon as you fill your bird feeder, before they bite into your power lines. Squirrels have a daytime feeding habit.

WHAT TO LOOK FOR: Half-eaten acorns, arcing household wiring.

TIPS TO INCREASE LIKELIHOOD OF SEEING: Put a bird feeder out. Squirrel calls are commercially available; one of the cheapest methods is to rub two pennies together.

OLD DIET: In Colonial times, the gray squirrel had a threepence price on its head for its damage to corn and wheat crops. Remembering its roots, the squirrel prefers wild tree fruits and nuts—it's estimated that a squirrel can consume/waste/squirrel away up to fourteen pounds of pecans a month. Plant seeds, tulip bulbs, insects, greens, berries, bark, tree buds, and twigs come a distant second.

NEW DIET: Power lines, household wiring, barbecue grill hoses, school peanut butter sandwiches forbidden by adult mixed nuts, maple syrup pipelines, and when they have a song in their heart, baby songbirds. Bird seed, any bird seed. Mr. Peanut products, especially crunchy style.

FOR THOSE ON A SQUIRREL DIET: Cases of mad squirrel disease from eating squirrel brains have been reported in the Southeast. It doesn't take too much gray matter to prefer the large back legs for roasting.

OLD BEHAVIOR: Squirrels go out on a limb to get their preferred foods. Their teeth continue growing all their life, so they gnaw on anything just to keep sharp.

NEW BEHAVIOR: Squirrels are becoming very impatient with all the anti-squirrel devices used on bird feeders. Tilt-tops, baffles, angled rims, and caged feeders designed to "thwart" squirrels in their feeding are just new puzzles for the tree rodent; bird lovers are now using "last-resort" feeders, delivering a mild electric shock to "teach" squirrels a lesson. As anyone with relatives who've had shock therapy can attest, this treatment will only make them more squirrelly.

LIKELIHOOD OF SIGHTING IN THE NEW MILLENNIUM: One hundred percent.

FUTURE: Squirrels are the number-one revenue generator for animal nuisance companies. Don't think for one minute these businesses want to catch enough squirrels to even slow the population growth. Follow the money!

In a nutshell, squirrels know they are a rodent, but they are a rodent with a fluffy tail, almond-shaped eyes, and have little human-like hands that can take a peanut and live above ground, not below.

WHALE (gray)

ALIAS: Doesn't have one, doesn't need one

SCIENTIFIC NAME: *Eschrichtius robustus*

PERSONAL STATISTICS: Adults crack any scale known to man at thirty to forty-five tons, and bust the measuring tape at fifty feet.

WHERE TO VIEW: The best place is behind a harpoon in a really big boat, or it was until the International Whaling Commission's moratorium on commercial whaling in 1985. After 1985, bumping into them with a cruise boat during their semiannual migration along the West Coast. On the East Coast, the sightseeing boats bump so many whales, the mammals have big humps on their backs. The worst place is behind a harpoon in an indigenous canoe; or encrusted in Mexican lagoons, where *federales* moonlight distilling seawater for the salt to rim gringo margaritas.

WHEN TO VIEW: During their spring and fall migrations along the West Coast.

WHAT TO LOOK FOR: Blowholes and the blowhards aboard the Greenpeace and Sea Shepherd Conservation Society party boats.

TIPS TO INCREASE LIKELIHOOD OF SEEING: Marry a Macaw tribal member.

TIPS TO DECREASE LIKELIHOOD OF SEEING: Carry a harpoon in the boat.

OLD DIET: Amphipods (small bottom-dwelling animals).

NEW DIET: Small bottom-dwelling and large harpoon-throwing animals.

OLD BEHAVIOR: As a member of the sea-going mammal group that has contributed mightily to the wooden leg industry, the gray whale took the whaler community down a peg or two.

NEW BEHAVIOR: To take up enough space underwater to keep the Sea Shepherds afloat. Gray whales may choose a migration even further off-shore as the Macaw Indians of Washington State risk their lives or, more importantly, their hunting reputations exercising court-approved "harvest" rights. This coastal tribe is the only one whose nineteenth-century treaty with the United States government specifically preserved the right to hunt whales and who has permission to "harpoon" with .50 caliber exploding ammo.

LIKELIHOOD OF SIGHTING IN THE NEW MILLENNIUM: One hundred percent. Gray whales can live up to the ripe old age of sixty or more, provided there are no harpoons sticking in their neck. As a group, these bottom-feeding behemoths are rebounding nicely, over twenty thousand strong.

FUTURE: The gray whale's imposing size is not enough for them to be a media star, unless other bankrupt coastal tribes decide to read between the lines of their ancient treaties with the federal government. Once the elders of any tribe chooses their weapons, the local business community has a whale of a time.

The greatest danger to the gray whale is to be designated the California Gray Whale. The merchant nature of California-based "research foundations" was even too much for J. J., a gray whale once held captive by Sea World. Released back into the wild, this hand-raised whale rubbed off her satellite and radio tracking devices and is having a whale of a time, freer than Wee Willy, somewhere in the South Pacific.

WHALE (Orca)

ALIASES: Killer, Wolf of the Sea (National Geographic), fat-chopper, Willy and a few other captives: Keiko, Shamu (Seaworld), Namu (Seattle), and Moby Doll, the world's first captive orca, in Vancouver, British Columbia, in 1967.

SCIENTIFIC NAME: *Orcinus orca*

PERSONAL STATISTICS: Adult males weigh from nine thousand to sixteen thousand pounds, females from three thousand to eight thousand pounds. Adult males are from twenty to thirty feet in length, females from seventeen to twenty-four feet.

WHERE TO VIEW: General distribution is wherever warm, fuzzy images are sold on warm, fuzzy clothes. The best place is at the movies: *Free Willy* (1993), *Free Willy 2—The Adventure Home* (1995), *Free Willy 3—The Rescue* (1997), and *Set My Willy Free* (now being filmed at the White House). The worst place is at *Free Willy* gift shops.

WHEN TO VIEW: During normal aquarium hours.

WHAT TO LOOK FOR: *Free Willy* gift shops, limp dorsal fins.

TIPS TO INCREASE LIKELIHOOD OF SEEING: Visit any wonderful world of nature store.

OLD DIET: Seals, squid, herring, sting rays, salmon, sea lions, Wally the Penguin, gray whale calves, scuba divers, minke whales, gray whale pups, and—in packs—sperm whales.

NEW DIET: In captivity, pre-chewed steelhead trout. Keiko put on almost two thousand pounds in captivity. With shrinking pinepid populations, otters stuffed with abalone are getting a case of the willies.

OLD BEHAVIOR: Breaching and eating Flipper.

NEW BEHAVIOR: As slavish to Hollywood role models as those on the dry side of the observation glass, impressionable young wild orcas seek the safe sanctuary of the media stars. Deep-water elders are attacking sperm whales, competition for the short attention span of water-borne tourists.

LIKELIHOOD OF SIGHTING IN NEW MILLENNIUM: Uncertain. Keiko enjoyed captivity, particularly *Andy Griffith Show* reruns, but his reintroduction to the wild is underway. Mechanical stand-ins will star in *Free Willy IV—The Abandonment.*

LIKELIHOOD OF SIGHTING ANOTHER MAJOR TOURIST ATTRACTION SET FREE IN THE NEW MILLENNIUM: Zero percent.

FUTURE: Orca whales are found in all the oceans and as the marine equivalent of the panda bear, on apparel, dinnerware, bedding, slumber bags, candles, cake toppers, video games, and other expensive locations. The rampant commercialism is enough to give most parents the willies.

Similar to the effort to "tame" wolves in our perceptions, Willy wonks work very hard to disassociate from the "killer" designation, unless they work for Time-Life nature snuff-film videos.

WOLF (gray)

ALIASES: Timber wolf, Lobo

SCIENTIFIC NAME: *Canus lupus;* in cattle-raising country, *Canus wheresthebeeficus*

PERSONAL STATISTICS: Adult males weigh up to 175 pounds and the female around 60 pounds; both are four to six feet in length.

WHERE TO VIEW: General distribution is wherever wolf sweatshirts are worn. The best place is in the Yellowstone National Park Gray Wolf Petting Zoo, at North Carolina State University, in *Wolf* (1994) where Jack Nicholson displays the predatory editor behavior long suspected by authors, in northern Minnesota/Michigan/Wisconsin/Idaho, wherever Friends of the Wolf howl on a full moon. The worst place is on image apparel with the pack "in a pensive winter moment" or as a reminder "to seize the moment" or "to inspire keen observation before taking action," all part of being "at home with nature."

WHEN TO VIEW: Minnesota timber wolves have eaten most of the loose animals in the northern part of the state, so they are playing hooky to move toward the cities to play hooky, hockey.

WHAT TO LOOK FOR: Empty coyote skins.

WHAT TO LISTEN FOR: Distressed coyotes and the loud smacking of wolf lips.

TIPS TO INCREASE LIKELIHOOD OF SEEING: Blow on a distressed rabbit call, which will attract tasty coyotes, too. To attract a wolf in Yellowstone National Park, wear and use your touch-activated 'Howling' wolf shirt. No need to tuck that shirt in for the soon-to-arrive alpha wolf. To decrease the likelihood of being bit by a rabid wolf, "Wake not a sleeping wolf." (William Shakespeare, *Henry IV*)

OLD DIET: The Three Little Pigs, Little Red Riding Hood, The Little Boy Who Cried Wolf, fifteen to twenty deer a year. It should be noted that the Big Bad Wolf would have preferred to eat a coyote than Little Red Riding Hood. Even a red fox, another competitor for wolf food, would have been preferred.

NEW DIET: In these gentler times, it's no longer necessary to wolf down food. Coyotes are meant for a leisurely dining.

OLD BEHAVIOR: As villain in *Little Red Riding Hood* and *The Three Little Pigs*, barking at the moon, howling with Wolfman Jack on the radio. It's illegal to howl back at the wolves in Yellowstone, something about them being Canadian and not knowing American swear words. If you howl back at coyotes, a wolf may come join you for dinner, you being the entrée.

In his book *Never Cry Wolf*, Farley Mowat claimed that unlike humans, wolves don't kill for fun. Obviously, Mowat hasn't barked lately with the national park coyotes.

NEW BEHAVIOR: Under the protection of the Endangered Species Act, the wolf rewrites Prokofiev's *Peter and the Wolf*, a tale of how a little boy and his three pals—a bird, a duck, and a cat—outwitted and captured the wicked wolf for the zoo. Less likely to hunt in packs in the city because the prey is so stupid. Wolf-whistling at the pretty suburban canines near development construction sites.

In the Montana version of the Good Book, Chapter Isaya: "The wolf lies down full of the lamb, the kid, and the yearling, and the calf together, evermore, without end, woof, burp, amen!"

LIKELIHOOD OF SIGHTING IN THE NEW MILLENNIUM: One hundred percent. The image of the lone wolf will continue as a role model having morphed into an American icon of rugged individualism. However, wildlife biologists know that a lone male wolf is most likely a loser, one who has left the pack and not always by choice. The alpha male wolf of the pack has it best— he's the only one who mates with the alpha babe and, if he wanted, the beta babe, too. Ditto for the rest of the alphabet. The other males are furry court eunuchs.

FUTURE: Once the U.S. Park Service promised Montana cattle ranchers to ring the park with an electronic pet containment system or "invisible fence," Canadian gray wolves were reintroduced into Yellowstone, causing local coyotes one link down the predator chain to howl unfair practices and Little Red Riding Hoods to check into Old Faithful Lodge. If these aliens act unwolflike by leaving rancher stock alone during the trial period of high public scrutiny, the Park Service will replace their visitor visas with resident green cards. Immediately following the swearing-in ceremony at park headquarters, the newly naturalized citizens will be free to concentrate on more wolf-like behavior and seriously rearrange the coyote social structure and livestock community. No two-legged creature is still afraid of the Big Bad Wolf. Silk-screened on sand-washed apparel, the gray wolf is the poster canine of the new millennium. Friends of the Wolf offer sponsorships of individual wolves, which included a gilt certificate suitable for framing, a chunk of coyote fur, and a four-pack of chocolate-covered wolf scat.

REPTILES

In the earliest and most popular of early times, reptiles ruled the land, sea, and air. Any student of contemporary politics recognizes that lineage in the dinosaur subspecies that currently rule at the federal level; when the snakes in our political high grass put the bite on the American taxpayer, the effects can be much more toxic and longer lasting. As issues of real national importance surface on the floor of either chamber, in the regulatory agencies, or the "de-briefing" rooms of the White House, vertebrates become invertebrates in remarkable reverse evolution. With the boomer population aging quickly in the new millennium, that era's pop culture dinosaurs continue to lay chemically altered eggs at concert revivals. When voters dump the humorless liberals, Republican party animals and the American alligator will no longer be so endangered. But look out snakes and turtles! These quiet residents will need to burrow deeper to escape an aggressive corporate economy, not to mention the need for more snake-oil in the resource shell-game. Luckily, turtle meat tastes more like the less-preferred dark chicken meat. There is little to be thought of as toothsome here. Except maybe a little gator tail.

ALLIGATOR

ALIASES: El Largato, Ramon, Albert

SCIENTIFIC NAME: *Alligator mississipiensis*

PERSONAL STATISTICS: Adults usually weigh 450 to 500 pounds; eight hundred pounders are usually full of pets; thousand pounders are usually full of large pets. They stretch from thirteen to eighteen feet, including a six- to eight-foot-long tail.

WHERE TO VIEW: General distribution is the swampy golf course communities of Southeastern United States. The best place to view the hide is in cowboy boots, belts, and handbags, the heads as ashtrays, and in *The Alligator People* (1959), *Alligator* (1980), and *Alligator II: The Mutation* (1991). The worst place is poking their noses out of your commode, above the sewers of New York City where they grow to abnormal sizes feeding on growth hormone-laced lab animal carcasses. If you are up to your ass in these urban alligators, you won't have time to remind yourself that your initial

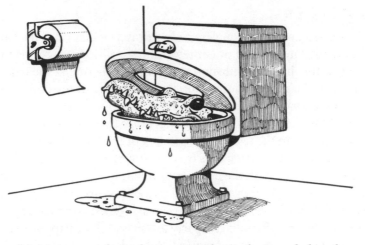

objective was to drain the swamp. Also in the Everglades where the Giant Gator lives, and your child's wading pool.

WHEN TO VIEW: At night in the swamp, with a small dog paddling behind the boat.

WHAT TO LOOK FOR: Empty small dog collars.

TIPS TO INCREASE LIKELIHOOD OF SEEING: Send your miniature poodle out to get the newspaper in Southern Florida.

OLD DIET: Frogs, insects, shrimp, crayfish, adult fish (particularly the bony garfish), and small wild mammals.

NEW DIET: Dachshunds, Chihuahuas, Shih Tzus, and the fish and birds that ate their little brothers and sisters.

OLD BEHAVIOR: Enjoying the confusion with the thinner-nosed, man-eating crocodiles, even claiming credit for Captain Hook's hand. Older alligators can be fooled—witness Charles's flight over the head of the Grandfather of All Alligators in the magical *Freddy Goes to Florida* by Walter R. Brooks.

NEW BEHAVIOR: Reminiscing about the old Gator-Aid Concerts while shedding crocodile-sized tears.

LIKELIHOOD OF SIGHTING IN THE NEW MILLENNIUM: One hundred percent in their Southern habitat.

FUTURE: Ten years after being placed on the endangered list, the *el Legarto* population has rebounded to nearly two million animals and is now considered completely recovered. Once thought to be reclusive, the American alligator enjoys swimming in flood-control canals, golf course water holes, and community wading pools. The Florida Game and Fresh Water Commission receives over ten thousand alligator nuisance complaints from frightened citizens every year and the state has mandated that any alligator over four feet long that's not afraid of humans must be destroyed. Once the children of the adults wrestled in alligator prison farms reach full size, the nuisance calls are expected to increase. See you later, alligator.

SNAKE
(diamondback rattlesnake)

ALIAS: Rattler

SCIENTIFIC NAME: *Crotalus adamanteus* in the East; *Crotalus atrax* in the West

PERSONAL STATISTICS: Adult weight fluctuates up and down and all around, but no matter what it still measures out to seven feet long.

WHERE TO VIEW: The best place is in a serpentarium. The worst place is as a skeptical initiate into a snake-worshipping cult.

WHEN TO VIEW: Dawn to dusk.

WHAT TO LOOK FOR: Discarded snake skin (make darned sure the skins are discarded).

TIPS TO INCREASE LIKELIHOOD OF SEEING: Putting your hands where they are not supposed to be.

OLD DIET: Birds and bird eggs, rodents, and frogs.

NEW DIET: Your pooch, your cat, your unruly children.

OLD BEHAVIOR: Waiting to bite through any pointy-toed snakeskin boot.

NEW BEHAVIOR: Still waiting to bite through any pointy-toed snakeskin boot.

LIKELIHOOD OF SEEING IN THE NEW MILLENNIUM: One hundred percent.

FUTURE: Of the one-hundred-plus snake species in North America, only nineteen are poisonous. Since fewer than ten persons die each year from bites of all native snakes, rattlers aren't perceived as a direct threat to urban sprawl. What isn't commonly understood is that non-fatal snake bite reactions range, in the language of the *American Journal of Emergency Medicine,* from "minor" to "major" outcomes. The latter outcomes should be of interest to urban sprawlers: life-threatening symptoms and significant residual disabilities ranging from repeated seizures, respiratory compromise that required intubation, ventricular tachycardia with hypertension, cardiac or respiratory arrest, esophageal stricture, and disseminated intravascular coagulation.

TURTLE (snapping)

ALIASES: The Great Turtle; with less snap—Franklin; with less bite—Leonardo, Raphael, Donatello, Michaelangelo

SCIENTIFIC NAME: *Chelydra serpentina*

PERSONAL STATISTICS: Adults weigh from twenty-five to fifty pounds, occasionally up to sixty-five pounds. Adult length is from ten to eighteen inches, occasionally up to three feet long.

WHERE TO FIND: General distribution is Central and Eastern United States, west to the Rockies. The best place is migrating to a nesting area; best not disturb this activity unless you want to see the reptilian version of *Jaws*. Other turtles are seen easily racing bunnies; best not interrupt this activity unless you wish to interrupt a hare-brained fable. The worst place is wading in Southern waters, the home of the alligator snapping turtle—the world's largest (up to two hundred pounds) freshwater turtle.

WHEN TO VIEW: In the spring when they move to their nesting sites and during their summer migration.

WHAT TO LOOK FOR: It's a snap—drags marks on a dirt road.

TIPS TO INCREASE LIKELIHOOD OF SEEING: Dig up their eggs.

OLD DIET: Ducklings, fish, carrion, vegetation, more ducklings, insects, crustaceans, oh, what else? amphibians, too.

NEW DIET: Add the fingers of those who try to pick these turtles up by their feet to the above list.

OLD BEHAVIOR: Lying in wait, hoping "the sweet asses" of the International Association of the Turtles go into hibernation.

NEW BEHAVIOR: Even fewer snap decisions.

LIKELIHOOD OF SIGHTING IN THE NEW MILLENNIUM: One hundred percent. The likelihood of being served Snapping Turtle in the new millennium is around 5 percent. At the old Dew Drop Inn in St. Cloud, Minnesota, deep-fried snapping turtle was served in place of fish for Catholics on Friday. Only conservative clerics maintain that tradition.

FUTURE: A snapper's preferred environments are the water sports vacation spots of the future: large impoundments and oxygen-depleted waters with pollutants that stimulate abnormal vegetable growth.

    The snapper is our best bet against pari-mutuel turtle racing, should they be introduced to the radioactive slime in NYC sewers, COWABUNGA!

HOW TO AVOID THE WILDLIFE OF THE NEW MILLENNIUM

Use Modern Techniques of Negative Reinforcement to Let Them Know They Are Not Welcome

The Outer Perimeter

1. Lay out fence, three strands high, the first ten inches from ground charged with direct current from major power source. Atomic is okay.
2. Paint mixture of peanut butter and oil slurry on fence wire.
3. At first sight or sound of wildlife, throw switch.

The Inner Perimeter

1. Remove welcome mat (most important).
2. Remove all outside feeders.
3. Destroy all vegetation and/or replace with thorny/animal noxious plants and/or concrete.
4. Drain bird feeder, hot tub, swimming pool, and pond. Cover all access to ground water with anti-freeze.
5. Turn up thermostats in all rooms in all buildings to 100 degrees Fahrenheit. Fur-bearers that can't stand the heat will leave your kitchen.
6. Connect white noise generator to your stereo and crank volume knob hard right.
7. If all this doesn't work, pull out Louisville Slugger, Joe DiMaggio model.

Any wild animal that survives this personal attention deserves your place in the new millennium!

AFTERWORD

WILD ANIMALS don't belong in our consumer-based society. They worry enough about being consumed within their own society. Wild animals can't even coexist with a population escaping the big cities. They need to exist on their own terms, yet we persist in making them common and correct so a "relationship" can develop and "management" can support our relentless population sprawl.

Unfortunately, as David Quammen notes in his well-thought *Wild Thoughts from Wild Places*, a "relentless replacement of wild populations by feral ones, rare species by weedy ones, inconvenient beasts by convenient ones, is a lamentably broad trend." Will there be real "wildlife" in the new millennium? Perhaps, but only in isolated pockets. The only way we could quarantine wild animals faster is if they somehow learned to smoke cigarettes in our brand-new, brave new smoke-free world. Will animal life be forever altered by significant human contact? There will certainly be less room for "wildlife" on the flatlands and foothills surrounding Atlanta, St. Louis, Orlando, Cincinnati, and other cities of rapid suburban growth. All the tiny urban backyard "nature-scapes" jammed with expensive "nature" merchandise to attract and harbor the photogenic few who rely too readily on human handouts cannot replace the rich, wild, less predictable biodiversity of the original landscape.

A Hollywood-size smile is destined to be the single most important qualification to survive in a hopped-up new century of "buzz," posturing, infotainments, and narcissistic self-love.

149

Animal species, too, will be judged on appearance, since performance will seem to have been modified to fit an unsuitable and unhealthy urban environment. For the urban animals with the shortest memories of the wild, and futures of short-term growth and ignored long-term consequences, the here and thereafter will be a wild one.

The Animal Kingdom Come!

Acknowledgments

MY SINCERE THANKS to Marilyn Hoffman and her teaching friends for the reintroduction to children's literature. My appreciation and understanding of the role of animals in muddled memories of growing up was also refreshed by William Kotzwinkle's *The Bear Went Over the Mountain*, the reissue of the great *Freddy the Pig* adventures by Walter R. Brooks, Nick Park's zoo animal interviews in *Creature Comforts*, the quiet friendship of Piglet and Poo and the noisier pals, Calvin & Hobbes, Ren and Stimpy's Untamed World (especially the horny-billed Chihuahua), the above-the-line humor in *Over the Hedge*, and *Babe* in the country and city. Of course, the author's heart belongs to Dorothy, Buck's loyal hunting pig. Anyone interested in the natural world should be familiar with David Quammen's work, and Steve Bodio's views on responsible stewardships with a personal dimension deserve close attention.

My sympathies go to the animal field advocates, professional biologists trying to balance the needs of wildlife management and a pressing need to educate a distracted public. My concerns are for today's parent trying to preserve and pass along worthy memories.

Pictured above are illustrator J. Angus "Sourdough" McLean and author "Buck" Peterson, both considered out standing in their own fields (or even better, further afield), amid the bucolic splendor at the base of Mount Mille Lacs, near Buck's Wilderness Lodge and Advanced Plucking Center in Northernmost Minnesota. The author's famous hunting pig, Dorothy, is never far from her master's side or lunch pail. The bird flew in just for the day.